TOP 10
CORSICA

RICHARD ABRAM

DK

EYEWITNESS TRAVEL

Left **L'Oriu de Cani rock formation** Right **Porto-Pollo beach, Golfe de Valinco**

LONDON, NEW YORK,
MELBOURNE, MUNICH AND DELHI
www.dk.com

Printed and bound in China by
South China Printing Co. Ltd

First published in Great Britain in 2012
by Dorling Kindersley Limited,
80 Strand, London WC2R 0RL
A Penguin Random House Company

14 15 16 17 10 9 8 7 6 5 4 3 2 1

**Copyright 2012, 2014 © Dorling
Kindersley Limited, London**

Reprinted with revisions 2014

A CIP catalogue record is available from the
British Library

ISBN 978 1 4093 2642 7

Within each Top 10 list in this book, no
hierarchy of quality or popularity is implied.
All 10 are, in the editor's opinion,
of roughly equal merit.

MIX
Paper from
responsible sources
FSC www.fsc.org FSC™ C018179

Contents

Corsica's Top 10

The information in this DK Eyewitness Top 10 Travel Guide is checked regularly.
Every effort has been made to ensure that this book is as up-to-date as possible at the time of going to press. Some details, however, such as telephone numbers, opening hours, prices, gallery hanging arrangements and travel information are liable to change. The publishers cannot accept responsibility for any consequences arising from the use of this book, nor for any material on third party websites, and cannot guarantee that any website address in this book will be a suitable source of travel information. We value the views and suggestions of our readers very highly. Please write to: Publisher, DK Eyewitness Travel Guides, Dorling Kindersley, 80 Strand, London WC2R 0RL, or email travelguides@dk.com

Left **Capo Pertusato** Centre **Aiguilles de Bavella** Right **Ceramic ware, Pigna**

LANCASHIRE COUNTY LIBRARY	
3011812929896 8	
Askews & Holts	10-Jun-2014
914.499048 ABR	£7.99
NST	

Left **Maquis vegetation covering the cliffs of Cap Corse** Right **Ste-Lucie de Tallano**

Key to abbreviations
Adm *admission*

CORSICA'S TOP 10

TOP10 Corsica's Highlights

Corsica encapsulates the best the Mediterranean has to offer. Protected by strict environmental laws, its coastline has escaped the kind of development that has subsumed the Rivieras, while the forests, gorges and crumbling villages of the interior have altered little in centuries. The island also preserves a wealth of historic monuments, ranging from the Bronze Age menhirs of the Torréen people to spectacular Genoese Citadelles.

1 Ajaccio

Beneath the Mediterranean chic of its high-rise outskirts, the capital of Corsica has retained a strong historic accent, underlined by the presence of the remarkable Palais Fesch – a storehouse of priceless Renaissance art *(see pp8–11)*.

2 Golfe de Valinco

Wild hillsides sweep from the shores of the Golfe de Valinco, where a string of white-sand beaches line a shoreline dotted with small resorts and, just inland, extraordinary prehistoric sites *(see pp12–13)*.

3 Le Sartenais

Head here if you are searching for wilderness. Standing stones are strewn over a landscape of pristine Mediterranean scrub, edged by a succession of remote beaches *(see pp14–15)*.

4 Bonifacio

The striated chalk cliffs of Bonifacio are southern Corsica's iconic sight. A perfectly preserved Genoese *haute ville* (upper town) perches on the cliffs above the translucent turquoise water *(see pp16–17)*.

L'Île-Rousse
Lumio
Calvi 8
Pigna
Argentella
Calenzana
Ascc
Galéria
Haut-Asco
Bárghiana
Partinello
Calasima
Golfe de Porto 10
Porto
Évisa
Piana
Soccia
Guag
Vico
Cargèse
Rezza
Sagone Tiuccia Arro
Bocogn
Golfe de Sagone
Ucciar
Peri
Ajaccio 1
Bastelicaccia
Golfe d'Ajaccio
Cauro
Portigliolo
Casalabriva
Aullè
Porto-Pollo
Proprian
Golfe de Valinco 2
Le Sartenais 3
Sart
Grossa
Tizzano
de
Roccapina

Mediterrane Sea

Preceding pages **The Citadelle, Bonifacio**

Bastia 5

Facing Tuscany across the Tyrrhenian Sea, Bastia has a more chaotic, Italian feel than its southern rival Ajaccio, at its most pervasive in the picturesque Vieux Port *(see pp18–19)*.

Cap Corse 6

Lovely views of the distant Tuscan Islands lend this peninsula, due north of Bastia, a special atmosphere – best savoured with a glass of the local muscat wine *(see pp20–21)*.

St-Florent and the Nebbio 7

The pretty port of St-Florent is a world away from the bustle of Bastia. Travel across its gulf to swim in some of the Mediterranean's most dazzlingly turquoise coves *(see pp22–3)*.

Calvi 8

Calvi's weathered Genoese Citadelle presides over a lovely sweep of white sand, sparkling sea water and snow-streaked granite mountains *(see pp24–5)*.

Corte and its Hinterland 9

The mountain town of Corte occupies a grandiose setting. Its crow's nest Citadelle is dwarfed by vast escarpments and snowy peaks *(see pp26–7)*.

Golfe de Porto 10

Admire the breath-taking scenery of the northwest, where cliffs of red porphyry plunge into a deep blue gulf. Hop on a boat from Porto's marina to see the Calanches rock formations *(see pp28–9)*.

Tollare
Cap Corse 6
Centuri
Macinaggio
Pino
Luri
Minervio
Albo
Nonza
Erbalunga
Golfe de St-Florent
D80
Florent and the Nebbio 7
D81
Bastia 5
N193
ama
Pietralba
Borgo
La Canonica
N193
Vescovato
Ponte-Novo
Folelli
Ponte Leccia
San Nicolo
Sovéria
Prunete
Corte
Moita
Altiani
Spazzola
vivario Vezzani
Caterragio
Ghisoni
Aléria
Poggio di Nazza
Ghisonaccia
Pietrapola
ozzano
Travo
avo
Solaro
Solenzara
Bavella
Favone
Zonza
Conca
Fautea
arbini
Pinarello
Porto-Vecchio
Sotta
Santa Giulia
Tyrrhenian Sea
1 Bonifacio

— miles ⌐ 0 ⌐ km ⌐ 10

🔟 Ajaccio

With a backdrop of wild, granite mountains and lapis-blue sea, Ajaccio ranks among the most splendidly sited capitals in the Mediterranean. Travellers from Edward Lear to Guy de Maupassant were enthralled by its setting, and the imperial city remains an essential stop for visitors – not least because of its association with Napoleon, who was born and raised here. The Bonapartes' former residence lies in the heart of a grid of narrow, weather-worn alleys, where you can sip pastis at a pavement café while the locals take their afternoon passeghiata (walk), or enjoy fresh seafood straight off the boats.

Interior of Grand
Café Napoléon

🔆 Pick up the fun booklet for children – *Discover Ajaccio with Tino – A la découverte d'Ajaccio avec Tino* – from the Tourist Office.

🔆 Grand Café Napoléon is a great place for a cup of Corsican coffee *(see p75)*.

• Map H3 • Tourist Office: 3 Boulevard du Roi Jérome; 04955 15303; www.ajaccio-tourisme.com
• Salon Napoléonien: Place Foch; Map P2; 04955 15253; Open 9–11:45 am, 2–4:45pm (to 5:45pm in summer); Closed Sat–Sun in winter • Maison Bonaparte: Rue St Charles; Map P3;04952 14389; Open 10:30am–12:30pm, 1:15–6pm (to 4:30pm Oct–Mar); Closed Mon, 25 Dec, 1 Jan; Adm €7
• Palais Fesch: 50–52 Rue Cardinal Fesch; Map P1; 04952 62626; Open May–Sep: 10:30am–6pm Mon, Wed, Sat; noon–6pm Thu, Fri, Sun; Oct– Apr: 10am–5pm Mon, Wed, Sat, noon–5pm Thu, Fri, Sun; Adm €8

Top 10 Features

1. Îles Sanguinaires
2. The Citadelle
3. Farmers' Market
4. Salon Napoléonien
5. Les Millelli
6. Maison Bonaparte
7. Fishing Harbour
8. Palais Fesch
9. Ajaccio Cathedral
10. Cimetière

Îles Sanguinaires

One of Alphonse Daudet's most famous novellas, *Lettres de mon Moulin*, was inspired by a visit to this archipelago of exquisite islets, tapering into the sea from the northern tip of Ajaccio's gulf *(above)*.

The Citadelle
Originally built by the Genoese, Ajaccio's hexagonal Citadelle *(below)* juts into the bay next to St-François beach. The fortress is considered sacred by Corsicans for having housed resistance fighters in World War II.

Farmers' Market
Each weekday during the tourist season, producers from across the island descend on the Place Foch in front of the Town Hall to sell fragrant local honey, fresh maquis herbs and artisanal sausages *(above)*.

Salon Napoléonien
Napoleon's death mask is just one among dozens of quirky items of memorabilia on show at this small museum inside the Hôtel de Ville on Place Foch.

Maison Bonaparte
The Bonapartes lived in this house until Paolist rebels drove them into exile in 1793. The sofa on which Napoleon was born is the prize exhibit.

Palais Fesch
This former palace, now a museum, boasts a fine collection of Reniassance art. *Leda and the Swan*, a 16th-century painting by Paolo Veronese, is also on display *(right)*.

Ajaccio Cathedral
A brooding Delacroix painting of the Virgin holding the Sacred Heart sets a sombre tone for visits to this late-baroque cathedral *(below)*, where Napoleon was baptized.

Cimetière
The local bourgeoisie have long contended with each other to erect the most awe-inspiring tombs in the cemetery sprawling from Ajaccio's western fringe. The *cimetière* is a city in miniature, with rows of domed neoclassical mausoleums and marble memorial gardens. French singer and actor Tino Rossi (1907–83) is buried here.

Les Millelli
Nestled in an olive grove overlooking the city, Les Millelli was the Bonapartes' country retreat. Napoleon stayed here during his last visit to Ajaccio in 1799. The grounds make for an excellent picnic spot.

Fishing Harbour
Ajaccio's tiny fishing quay *(main image)*, just south of the marina, is a great place to visit early in the morning, when the night's catch is being landed against a backdrop of palms, yachts and giant ferries.

Napoleon and Corsica

Although born in Ajaccio, Napoleon spent his formative years in Paris, becoming a passionate advocate of the French Revolution, which did little to endear him to Pascal Paoli's nationalist regime back home. Having been chased into exile by Paoli's supporters, Napoleon shunned his homeland for good, returning only once, briefly, while en route to France after his Egyptian campaign.

Left **Courtyard** Centre **Gallery** Right *Virgin and Child with an Angel*, Botticelli

10 Palais Fesch, Musée des Beaux Arts

1 Titian's Portrait of a Man with a Glove

The jewel in the crown of the museum's collection, this exquisite portrait by the legendary Venetian artist Titian (c.1488–1576) demonstrates the subtle use of luminous tints for which he became renowned. It originally formed part of Louis XIV's collection in Versailles.

2 Botticelli's Virgin and Child with an Angel

Virgin and Child with an Angel is one of the finest in a series of devotional pictures painted by Sandro Botticelli (1445–1510), a great master of the early Renaissance. The Virgin's evocative expression makes the painting one of the loveliest works in the museum.

3 Tommaso's Mystical Marriage of Saint Catherine

The first painting that one discovers when beginning a visit to the Palais Fesch's Italian collection is this piece on wood, with its striking colours and golden backdrop. It is a fine example of early Renaissance art by Niccolò di Tommaso (c.1346–76).

4 Bernini's Portrait of a Young Man

One of the masters of the Italian baroque, Gianlorenzo Bernini (1598–1680) enjoyed an illustrious career as a sculptor and architect. He was also an

Portrait of a Man with a Glove, Titian

exceptional portrait painter, and sometimes worked with others close to him, as for this brooding, psychologically intense work.

5 Recco's Still Life with Fish and Lobster

Few visitors pass this still life by Neapolitan artist Giuseppe Recco (1634–95) without pausing in wonderment at its photo-realisitic quality.

6 Gaulli's Joseph Recites a Dream to His Brothers

Also known as Il Baciccio, Giovanni Battista Gaulli (1639–1709) was Bernini's protégé and a veteran of the Baroque style. This painting is presented in the museum's large gallery next to its twin *Joseph Recognised by His Brothers*. The subject of these pieces is taken from the Old Testament and relates to two episodes in the life of Joseph.

A Cardinal's Collection

Cardinal Joseph Fesch, Napoleon's stepuncle, owned a large personal fortune and had a great eye for a bargain, at a time when Europe's art markets were awash with loot plundered by the French armies. The result was the largest private collection of paintings and classical sculpture in the world – a total of 16,000 pieces spanning five centuries. After the Cardinal's death in 1839, 1,500 pieces were bequeathed to Ajaccio. However, Fesch's principal heir, Napoleon's elder brother Joseph, contested the will and before the ensuing legal wrangle could be resolved, the Bonapartes craftily sold off the finest works, including many great Dutch masters. Early Renaissance art of the "Quattrocento" period was, on the other hand, undervalued at the time, so that today's Fesch collection includes an array of 15th- and early-16th-century Italian masterpieces.

Joseph Fesch

Veronese's Leda and the Swan
This erotic painting by Paolo Veronese (1528–88) depicts a scene from Greek mythology in which Zeus seduces Leda (mother of Helen of Troy) – a recurrent motif in Renaissance paintings for its controversial subject matter.

Tura's Virgin Mary and Child with Saint Jerome and a Holy Martyr
This 15th-century painting by the Italian painter Cosmè Tura of Ferrara (c.1433–95) was bequeathed by Cardinal Fesch to the city of Ajaccio in 1839.

Gérard's Napoleon in Coronation Robes
François Gérard (1770–1837) painted all the leading figures of the Napoleonic period in France, especially the emperor himself, who is portrayed here at his most pompous. The work is the show stealer of the museum's Napoleonic collection.

Solimena's The Departure of Rebecca
Francesco Solimena (1657–1747) was one of the most prolific and successful figures of the baroque. His forté was dramatic biblical scenes such as this painting, which depicts Rebecca leaving for her marriage to Isaac.

The Departure of Rebecca, Solimena

Golfe de Valinco

The most southerly of the four great gulfs indenting Corsica's west coast, Valinco presents an arresting spectacle when seen from the high ridges enfolding it. Its vivid blue waters cleave into the heart of the Alta Rocca region, whose orange-roofed settlements cling to hillsides smothered in holm-oak forest and impenetrable maquis. People come here to laze on the gulf's necklace of sandy beaches, although some stupendous views are to be had from the ancient granite perched villages inland, which were the refuge of local inhabitants during the repeated pirate raids in the 15th and 16th centuries.

Holidaymakers at the beach, Porto-Pollo

🍴 One of the Valinco region's two main supermarkets is the Casino on the outskirts of Propriano.

🍴 A Madunnina on the main road midway between Propriano and Sartène serves wood-fired pizzas.

• Map J4
• Golfe de Valinco Tourist Office: Quai St-Erasme, Propriano; 04957 60149; www.lacoursedesorigines. com • Prehistoric Site of Filitosa: 10 km (6 miles) inland from Porto-Pollo on the D157; 04957 40091; Open Easter–Oct: 8am–sunset; Adm €7; www.filitosa.fr
• Gulf Cruises: Promenades en mer à Propriano; Port de Plaisance; 06125 49928; Mid-May–mid-Oct; Adm €40 (half-day excursion), €26 (sunset cruise)
• Bains de Caldanes: D148 Route de Granacce; Map K5; 04957 70034; Call for opening times; Adm €4

Top 10 Features

1. Propriano
2. Ste-Lucie de Tallano
3. Col de Siu
4. Porto-Pollo
5. Filitosa
6. Gulf Cruises
7. Fozzano
8. Plage de Cupabia
9. Campomoro
10. Bains de Caldanes

Propriano
1 A sleepy village out of season *(main image)*, Propriano transforms into a bustling resort and ferry port during the summer when visitors throng the stylish waterfront café terraces lining the town's marina.

Ste-Lucie de Tallano
2 Bucolic olive and almond groves surround this picturesque Alta Rocca village *(below)*. Taste cold-pressed oil in a mill outlet or watch *pétanque* players on a quintessentially Corsican, plane-shaded square.

Col de Siu
3 An unforgettable drive inland from Propriano on the little used D557 culminates in this lonely pass, visited by more goats than people. Scramble over the rocks for magnificent views of the gulf.

Porto-Pollo
4 This fishing village serves as the region's scuba-diving hub, as well as a springboard for trips to some hidden beaches nearby.

Filitosa
5 Corsica's world-famous prehistoric site is renowned for its collection of carved standing stones. Their eerily defiant features *(above)* were chiselled from granite phalluses 5,000 years ago.

Gulf Cruises
6 Excursion boats leave daily from Propriano marina *(above)* in the summer, calling at several coves, snorkelling hot spots and photogenic rock formations only reachable by sea. Some outfits offer romantic sunset cruises.

Fozzano
7 The real-life heroine of Prosper Mérimée's vendetta novel, *Colomba*, hailed from this tiny village. The granite tower-houses recall the hostile climate that prevailed here in the 19th century.

Campomoro
9 Spread behind a shell-shaped bay that is over-looked by a watchtower *(above)*, Campomoro is the perfect spot for a secluded, quiet vacation.

Bains de Caldanes
10 One of Valinco's quirkier attractions is this tiny hot spring *(right)*, 6 km (4 miles) from Ste-Lucie de Tallano. Its waters bubble at an invigorating 40°C (104°F).

Plage de Cupabia
8 Valinco's loveliest beach is the place to sidestep the summer crowds. Hidden over the hill from Porto-Pollo, it lies beyond the range of day-tripping Ajaccians, in a gloriously wild setting.

Vendetta in Corsica

Corsica is infamous for the blood feuds that wracked the island in past centuries. Valinco was the worst affected of all the regions. You only have to look at the forbidding appearance of many old houses, with their fortified rooftops and absence of ground-floor doorways, to get a sense of how pervasive the violence was. Fozzano is a prime example – its feud formed the backdrop to Prosper Mérimée's 19th-century block-buster, *Colomba*.

Le Sartenais

Coastal wilderness is a rarity in the Mediterranean these days, especially if it is endowed with sublime beaches. However, the southwest of Corsica, a region of windswept rocky shores and unbroken scrubland, has remained astonishingly untrammelled. Forced out by pirates and the collapse of the wine industry, its inhabitants left the maquis a century or so ago to the ghosts of their prehistoric ancestors, whose tombs and standing stones still litter the countryside. Roads will only take you so far hereabouts: this is one area you will need solid shoes and lots of bottled water to experience to the maximum.

Cala di l'Avena beach, Tizzano

🚗 If you have hired a car, remember that your rental agreement may not cover trips down unpaved tracks.

🍽 A great spot for lunch serving local specialities is the Bergerie d'Acciola *(see p83)*, on the roadside between Sartène and Roccapina.

• Map J5
• Tourist Office: 14 Cours Soeur Amélie; 04957 71540; www.lacoursedesorigines.com
• Musée Départemental de Préhistoire Corse et d'Archéologie: Rue Croce, Sartène; 04957 70109; Open Jun–Sep: 10am–6pm daily; Oct–May: 9am–noon, 1:30–5pm Mon–Fri; Closed public hols; Adm €4; www.prehistoire-corse.org • Domaine Saparale: 5 Cours Bonaparte, 20100 Sartène; 04957 71552; Visits by appt only • Site Archeologique de Cauria, RD48; 04952 91300

Top 10 Features

1. Sartène
2. Musée Départemental de Préhistoire Corse et d'Archéologie
3. Plage de Roccapina
4. Site Archeologique de Cauria
5. Alignement de Palaggiu
6. Dolmen de Fontanaccia
7. Plage d'Erbaju
8. Vallée de l'Ortolo
9. Tizzano and Cala di l'Avena
10. Sentier des Douaniers

Sartène
"The most Corsican of Corsican towns" is how Merimée described Sartène *(above)* in the 19th century. Its medieval granite buildings retain a dark undertone, reflected in the ancient Easter U Catenacciu parade.

Musée Départemental de Préhistoire Corse et d'Archéologie
This museum houses the finest collection of prehistoric artifacts on the island, some of them stretching right back to the early Neolithic age. It is an ideal primer for tours of this region's standing-stone sites *(above)*.

Plage de Roccapina
Radiant white sand, clear turquoise water, pristine maquis and rock outcrops combine to scintillating effect at Roccapina beach *(main image)*.

Site Archeologique de Cauria
This Neolithic archeological site holds the Stantari and Rinaghju alignments, with 22 phallic menhirs amid the maquis south of Sartène.

Alignement de Palaggiu

This is Corsica's largest collection of standing-stones, where 250 statue-menhirs cluster in a clearing *(right)*.

Dolmen de Fontanaccia

Known to locals as "The Devil's Forge", this late-megalithic burial chamber comprises six huge boulders topped by a slab. It is best viewed in the warm light of the setting sun.

Plage d'Erbaju

Clamber to the top of the headland overlooking Roccapina, crowned with a crumbling watch-tower and rock outcrop resembling a recumbent lion, to pick up the path to beautiful, deserted Erbaju beach.

Vallée de l'Ortolo

Overlooked by grey-granite cliffs, this empty valley just south of Sartène encapsulates the region's austere beauty *(above)*. Visit the Domaine Saparale vineyard to savour the valley's vintage wines.

Tizzano and Cala di l'Avena

Huddled around an inlet hemmed in by boulder-studded hills, the village of Tizzano is among the island's most remote fishing jetties. It is worth a visit primarily for the spectacular Cala di l'Avena beach nearby.

Sentier des Douaniers

The former Genoese custom-officers' path is now a world-class coast walk. It takes you along the rugged Sartenais shoreline via a non-stop parade of wild beaches, turquoise coves and the lonely Senetosa watchtower *(below)*.

U Catenacciu

Nothing conveys the aura of secrecy surrounding Corsican culture like the Easter processions of hooded penitents. Among these macabre parades, U Catenacciu, held on Good Friday in Sartène, is the oldest and most overtly sinister. The identity of the red-robed "Grand Pénitent" is kept a secret as the role perennially appeals to prominent mafiosi and fugitives from justice.

⑩ Bonifacio

Bonifacio is Corsica's foremost visitor attraction and, despite all the commotion in high season, more than merits the distinction. Spread over the top of a long, narrow promontory that is encircled on three sides by sheer chalk escarpments, the medieval Genoese haute ville (upper town) looks on one side across the straits to Sardinia and on the other over its secluded harbour, a port mentioned by Homer in The Odyssey. Aside from wandering around the ancient alleyways of the Citadelle, the other unmissable activity here is taking a boat trip for a view of the fabled white cliffs from water level.

Ticket office for excursions, Bonifacio

🎟 Except in high season, the ticket prices quoted by touts for the boat trips in the marina will always drop if you haggle.

🍴 For a money-saving snack, try the Spar Supermarket just east of the Quai Comparetti.

• Map K7
• Tourist Office: 2 Rue Fred Scamaroni; 04957 31188; www.bonifacio.fr
• Escalier du Roi d'Aragon: Haute Ville, Bonifacio; 04957 31188; Open Apr–Nov 9am–8pm; Adm €2.50
• Boat trips from Bonifacio marina, Promenades en Mer de Bonifacio, Port de Bonifacio: 04951 09750; Adm €15 (sea caves), Îles Lavezzi – 1-hour tour €17.50, longer tour €35

Top 10 Features

1. Quai Comparetti
2. Chapelle Roch
3. Montée Rastello
4. Escalier du Roi d'Aragon
5. Ste-Marie-Majeure
6. Beaches Around Bonifacio
7. Rue du Palais de Garde
8. Porte de Gênes
9. Boat Trips
10. Cimetière des Marins

Quai Comparetti
The café-restaurants of the Quai Comparetti are the perfect place to soak up the atmosphere of Bonifacio's marina, with its constant traffic of excursion boats and millionaires' yachts *(above)*.

Montée Rastello
This flight of stone steps leads from the port to a raised balcony just below the entrance to the Citadelle, where there is a matchless view of the famous "Grain de Sable" rock stack and cliffs.

Escalier du Roi d'Aragon
Get a hands-on experience of Bonifacio's chalk cliffs with a hike down this flight of 187 steps *(right)*, hewn from rock in medieval times, to reach a hidden freshwater well.

Chapelle Roch
This tiny shrine at the head of Montée Rastello is where Bonifacio's last plague victim died in the epidemic of 1518. Steps lead down to some superb snorkelling sites.

5 Ste-Marie-Majeure
Relics of the True Cross, said to have been donated by Emperor Constantine's mother St Helena, after she was saved from a shipwreck in the straits, number among the treasures enshrined in Bonifacio's historic church *(above)*.

6 Beaches Around Bonifacio
The chalky soils of the Bonifacio area have helped create some of the whitest, softest sand in all the Mediterranean. The beaches are at their most alluring in Sperone, Pianterella and Rondinara.

7 Rue du Palais de Garde
Multi-storeyed tenements with estucheon-embellished doorways flank this medieval street *(above)*. Residents still use winches to lift supplies to upper floors.

9 Boat Trips
Hop on a boat *(above)* to see Bonifacio's white cliffs and *haute ville* at their most resplendent. Launches also take in the exquisite Îles Lavezzi.

8 Porte de Gênes
In Genoese times, this turreted gateway, with its impressive drawbridge, served as the only entrance to the Citadelle. Beyond it, breathtaking sea views are to be had from the terrace of the Jardins des Véstiges.

Cimetière des Marins 10
At the far western tip of the promontory lies a walled cemetery *(right)* containing the fancily decorated tombs of deceased Bonifacians.

The Wreck of the Sémillante
They might look gorgeous on a sunny day, but the Straits of Bonifacio rank among the most fickle waterways in the world, with notoriously unpredictable currents and volatile weather. In 1885, the troop carrier *Sémillante* ran aground off the Îles Lavezzi while en route to the Crimea. An obelisk on the western-most islet commemorates the tragedy, in which 773 people lost their lives.

TOP 10 Bastia

Bastia is Corsica's commercial capital, with a more upbeat, big-city feel than Ajaccio. Since Genoese times, its nucleus has been a picturesque quarter of ramshackle old tenements, whose buttressed walls and cobbled alleyways radiate from a well-sheltered harbour. The twin bell towers of the St-Jean-Baptiste chuch are the town's emblematic landmark. Behind the Vieux Port, 18th-century boulevards yield to an amphitheatre of high-rise suburbs looking out to sea. The constant to and fro of ferries remind you that Italy is just across the water and its influence over Bastia's culture is ubiquitous.

Exterior of Musée de Bastia

🎬 **Bastia's art house cinema, the Studio, on Rue de la Miséricorde, regularly screens English-language releases.**

🍦 **Don't leave Bastia without sampling the delights of Chez Serge Raugi, Corsica's finest ice-cream maker.**

• Map F3
• Tourist Office: North end of Place St-Nicolas; Map P4; 04955 42040; www.bastia-tourisme. com • Place du Marché: Map P5; Open 7am–1pm Sat–Sun • Musée de Bastia: Place du Donjon, Citadelle; Map P6; 04953 10912; Open Apr–Oct: 10am–6pm (to 7:30pm Jul–mid-Sep) Tue–Sun, Nov–Mar: 9am–noon, 2–5:30pm Tue–Sat; Adm €5, €1 for garden visit; www.musee-bastia.com
• St-Jean-Baptiste: 4 rue du Cardinal Viale Préla; Map P5; 04955 52460; Open 8am–noon, 2–6pm Mon–Sat, Sun closed except 10am Mass

Top 10 Features

1. Place du Marché
2. Oratoire de l'Immaculée Conception
3. Place St-Nicolas
4. Boulevard Paoli
5. Musée de Bastia
6. Vieux Port
7. St-Jean-Baptiste
8. Scala Santa, Oratoire de Monserato
9. Cathedral Ste-Marie and Oratoire Ste-Croix
10. La Canonica

1 Place du Marché
This fresh-produce market is a source of local delicacies *(above)* as well as the perfect spot to people-watch over a leisurely coffee.

2 Oratoire de l'Immaculée Conception
This baroque chapel dates from 1611 and has an extra-vagant interior. Behind the high altar is one of Murillo's celebrated depictions of the Immaculate Conception.

3 Place St-Nicolas
Open to the sea on one side, Place St-Nicolas is where Bastiais come to wine, dine, stroll and play *pétanque* under the plane trees. A weekly flea market draws crowds here on Sunday mornings *(above),* open 6am–1pm.

4 Boulevard Paoli

Bastia's principal street is a grand thoroughfare, lined with lofty Napoleonic-era apartments and ritzy shops (left). The crowds usually lessen after lunch.

5 Musée de Bastia

The Citadelle's splendidly renovated Governors' Palace houses a state-of-the-art museum charting Bastia's evolution as a trade and artistic centre. Its collection includes part of Cardinal Fesch's famous hoard of Renaissance art.

6 Vieux Port

Head down to Bastia's old harbour (main image) at sunset, when the cafés ranged around it cast reflections in the limpid water. The tip of the harbour jetty provides the best viewpoint.

7 St-Jean-Baptiste

Built in the mid-1600s, this church was redecorated in baroque style in the following century. The nave displays marble decoration and gilded stucco work (above).

8 Scala Santa, Oratoire de Monserato

Bastia's most off-beat religious monument is a replica of the Holy Steps of St John Lateran's Basilica in Rome, which pilgrims traditionally ascend on their knees. Reach it from the Citadelle via the stepped Chemin des Fillipines.

9 Cathedral Ste-Marie and Oratoire Ste-Croix

This pair of majestic 15th-century rococo churches in Bastia's Citadelle hold miracle-working icons: the former a silver Virgin; the latter a blackened oak crucifix – "Christ des Miracles" – mysteriously fished out of the sea in 1428.

10 La Canonica

The stately La Canonica (below) is the finest of the 300 or so churches built by the Pisans across Corsica in the 12th century.

Bastia in World War II

Bastia witnessed the most intense battle fought on Corsican soil during World War II, when Kesselring's army fled through the city back to the Italian mainland. Ironically, the worst casualties were sustained the day after the Nazi evacuation. Due to a mix-up in the Allied command, a squadron of American B-52 bombers destroyed the Vieux Port just as its inhabitants were out celebrating in their newly liberated streets.

🔟 Cap Corse

Before the construction in the 19th century of the corniche that circles Cap Corse, the long, finger-like promontory running north from Bastia was practically inaccessible except via sea. To a large extent, Cap Corse still feels like a separate island. Wine was its raison d'être under the Genoese but production collapsed after the phylloxera epidemic of the early 1900s. However, the famous orange-blossom-scented muscat is still produced by a handful of growers, whose terraces spill from picturesque villages clinging to steep, fire-blackened mountain slopes.

Entrance to Le Pirate restaurant

🚗 Drivers of a nervous disposition should tour the cape's tortuous corniche in a clockwise direction, which ensures that they are always on the landward side of the road.

🍷 The apéritif of choice is the eponymous local tipple – Cap Corse – a fortified wine made using quinine (originally added as a malaria prophylaxis). Ask for "un Cap!"

- Map E2
- Tourist Office: Port de Plaisance, Macinaggio; 04953 54034; www.macinaggiorogliano-capcorse.fr
- Tourist Office: Port Toga, Pietrabugno; 04953 10232; www.destination-cap-corse.com
- Jardins Traditionnels du Cap Corse, Cepita (10 km from Luri): Map F2; 04953 50507; Open 9:30am–6:30pm; Adm €5; www.lesjardinstraditionnelsducapcorse.org

Top 10 Features

1. The Corniche
2. Erbalunga
3. Tour de Sénèque
4. Macinaggio
5. Centuri Port
6. Tollare
7. Nonza
8. Jardins Traditionnels du Cap Corse
9. Site Naturelle de la Capandula
10. Patrimonio

The Corniche
Built by Napoleon III, the corniche winds around the entire cape. The section just north of Bastia affords the best views, owing to its proximity to the Tuscan archipelago *(above)*.

Erbalunga
A Genoese watchtower stands guard over Erbalunga's harbour – the prettiest port on the cape's eastern shore *(main image)*. Affluent Bastiais drive up here to dine at the Michelin-starred Le Pirate restaurant *(see p99)*.

Tour de Sénèque
The Roman philosopher Seneca, exiled to a tower above the village of Luri *(above)*, found the sweeping views from his prison over the northern cape "desolate", but they are well worth the half-hour hike.

Macinaggio
On the northeastern tip of Cap Corse, Macinaggio and its blue marina have a remote feel. To get much further north, you have to strike out on foot, or jump on a boat.

Centuri Port

Centuri's cluster of neatly painted fishermen's houses, packed around the tiniest of harbours *(above)*, look almost too picturesque to be true. Its seafood restaurants keep the lobster boats busy all summer.

Tollare

A ribbon of tiny schist cottages clinging to the wave-lashed edge of Cap Corse, Tollare is the kind of place that makes you marvel at the resilience of its former inhabitants.

Nonza

Sweeping views across the Gulf of St-Florent extend from Nonza, a village perched on top of a rock pinnacle, whose surrounding cliffs plunge to a beach *(below)*.

Jardins Traditionnels du Cap Corse

Gardening enthusiasts will love this attraction on the eastern outskirts of Luri, set up to protect the vegetables, flowering plants and fruit trees that were formerly ubiquitous on the cape. Preserves are sold in the site shop.

Site Naturelle de la Capandula

A trio of idyllic beaches, backed by isolated Genoese watchtowers, provide the main incentive to follow the Sentier des Douaniers (old custom officers' path) through to this far-flung coastal nature reserve.

Patrimonio

Some of Corsica's finest wines originate in the undulating chalk terrain of Patrimonio, where stunning white cliffs frame views of the distant bay. The village church *(right)* is worth a stop here even if you are not a wine buff.

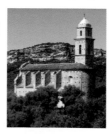

Les Maisons d'Américains

Many Cap Corsicans took to the colonies of south and central America to seek their fortune in the early 19th century. Having grown rich on gold prospecting or coffee planting, they returned to the land of their birth to end their days in grand mansions, whose fancy architecture echoed the source of their owners' wealth. Known locally as "les maisons d'Américains", the villas lend an exotic flavour to the cape.

🔟 St-Florent and the Nebbio

The Col de Teghime (Teghime Pass), separating Bastia from the Golfe de St-Florent, marks a dramatic shift in landscape, from the flat, intensively cultivated east coast to the more stark, mountainous terrain of the Nebbio – Corsica's proverbial "Land of Mists". By the time you reach the compact resort of St-Florent itself, whose slate-roofed houses hunker around the base of a Genoese Citadelle against a formidable backdrop of hills, the transition is complete. Press any further west and you venture into the Désert des Agriates, a sea of maquis and cacti fringed by empty beaches.

Café near St-Florent harbour

🚗 **Corse Plaisance,** south of the Place des Portes in St-Florent, is a handy source of holiday essentials, watersports paraphernalia and camping kits.

🍴 **All the patisseries** in St-Florent sell traditional local patties, or *bastelles*, filled with caramelized onions or chard spinach and cheese *(blétes).*

• Map E3
• Tourist Office: *Bâtiment Administratif, Route Principale 53, 20217; 04953 70604; www. corsica-saintflorent.com*
• *Santa Maria Assunta: 1 km (half a mile) northeast of La Place des Portes; Open Jul–Aug: 5–8pm; at other times, ask at the tourist office in St-Florent for the key; Adm €2*
• *Le Popeye Promenade en Mer, La Porte, Campo d'Elge, St-Florent; 04953 71907; Adm €16 Apr–Jul, €20 Aug–Sep*

Top 10 Features

1. Santa Maria Assunta
2. Place des Portes
3. The Citadelle
4. The Quayside
5. Plage du Loto
6. Tour de Mortella
7. Désert des Agriates
8. Plage de Saleccia
9. San Michele de Murato
10. Oletta

Santa Maria Assunta

Stroll up the lane from the square to reach the delightful Pisan Church of Santa Maria Assunta. Inside its honey-coloured walls rests a glass-sided coffin containing the relics of St Flor, a Roman legionnaire.

Place des Portes

The "three Ps" – *pétanque,* pastis and *passeggiata* are the chief pastimes on offer in St-Florent's main square, where a trio of terrace cafés compete for custom in nonchalant Corsican style.

The Quayside

St-Florent's marina entices a steady flow of sailing enthusiasts over from the Riviera. This explains the odd Michelin star among the row of pizzerias lined up on the quayside fronting the harbour *(main image).*

The Citadelle

The bastion on the hillock above the harbour *(below)* was built in 1439, bombarded by Nelson's fleet in 1794 and restored in 2000. The terrace has great views of the gulf.

Plage du Loto

Take a 15-minute boat cruise out across the gulf from St-Florent to the Plage du Loto *(above)*, whose turquoise shallows and white sand are patrolled by a herd of wild cows.

San Michele de Murato

Perched on a high terrace at the head of the Nebbio, this 13th-century chapel features chequered bands of green schist and creamy yellow marble *(above)*. Look out for the grotesque figures adorning the eaves.

Plage de Saleccia

A half-hour hike from Loto brings you to the wilder Plage de Saleccia. Take a boat ride, or swim in the sublime water (but watch out for tidal rips).

Oletta

Pisan sculpture embellishes the façade of the 18th-century Eglise St-André in Oletta, a typical Nebbio village set high in the hills *(below)*.

Tour de Mortella

This watchtower *(above)* on the western shore of the gulf was the one that inspired Nelson to build a string of lookalike "Martello Towers" along the southern coasts of Britain and Ireland.

Désert des Agriates

Hire mountain bikes from Casta to explore the trails crisscrossing this moonscape of dried-up river beds, cacti and maquis-shrouded hills.

Nelson in Corsica

A forgotten naval campaign in Corsica provided future admiral Horatio Nelson with some valuable tactical lessons. Nelson was dispatched to the island in 1793 as part of Lord Hood's fleet, charged with supporting Pascal Paoli's insurrection against the French. The attack on the garrison at St-Florent went well enough, but Calvi proved a much tougher nut to crack – eventually costing Nelson the sight of one eye.

Corsica's Top 10

TOP 10 Calvi

Calvi has been a ritzy seaside resort since the 1920s, when aristocratic refugees from the Côte d'Azur used to come here to pursue illicit affairs in clubs such as the legendary Chez Tao. Rising straight from the waves, Calvi's Citadelle is easily the most imposing of Genoa's former strongholds, presiding imperiously over the bay. The icing on the cake, though, are the mountains. In clear weather the snow-streaked Corsican watershed seems so close you could almost touch it – a vision all the more surreal for its proximity to the breathtakingly blue sweep of Calvi's gulf.

Trinighellu train trundling along the coastal track

The local train, known as "Trinighellu", provides a convenient way to reach one of the area's loveliest and least frequented beaches, Plage de Bodri, 5 km (3 miles) west of L'Île Rousse.

A fresh-produce market specializing in local cheese, charcuterie and preserves, is held every morning in the summer in the hall between Rue Clémenceau and Boulevard Wilson.

- Map B4
- Tourist Office: 97 Port de Plaisance; 04956 51667; www.balagne-corsica.com
- Ste-Marie-Majeure: Rue Clémenceau, Ville Basse; Open 8am–6pm
- St-Jean-Baptiste: The Citadelle; Open 9am–7pm
- Maison Colombe; 04956 51667; visit by appt only

Top 10 Features

1. Quai Landry
2. Calvi Marina
3. Ste-Marie Majeure
4. Calvi Beach
5. Maison Colomb
6. St-Jean-Baptiste
7. The Trinighellu
8. Notre Dame de la Serra
9. Calenzana
10. Lumio

Quai Landry
The café-restaurants lining the ritzy Quai Landry *(above)* upstage even those of St Tropez and Cannes. If à-la-carte is too pricey, buy a coffee and people-watch.

Calvi Marina
Some of the gleaming yachts moored in this marina have to be seen to be believed. The harbour pier affords splendid views of the waterfront and Citadelle.

Ste-Marie Majeure
The pastel-pink belfry of Ste-Marie Majeure *(right)* dominates the backstreets of Calvi's old town, where restaurant tables spill across terraces on a square and buskers serenade late revellers in summer.

Calvi Beach

Backed by shady pine forest, Calvi's beach *(right)* arcs in a curve of pale orange sand and turquoise water around the gulf's southern rim.

Maison Colomb
It is unlikely that it will ever be proved beyond doubt that this derelict cottage in the Citadelle was Columbus' birthplace, but until it is, the town is determined to take the credit.

St-Jean-Baptiste
This octagonal-domed cathedral is the culminating point of Calvi's Citadelle. A crucifix, which allegedly saw off the Turkish siege of 1553, is its prize possession.

Notre Dame de la Serra
The ultimate viewpoint over Calvi and its splendid gulf is from the terrace of this atmospheric hilltop church *(right)*. It can be reached in an hour's walk from the seafront, or by car via a backroad off the D81.

Calenzana
The start point of the GR20 *(see p46)* mountain trail, this village inland from Calvi centres on the baroque Église St-Blaise, noted for its 17th-century tabernacle.

The Trinighellu
Calvi's single-carriage tramway train, known as "Trinighellu" (little train), rattles several times daily along the beautiful Balagne coast as far as L'Île Rousse. It stops at a string of pretty beaches and off-track resorts *(see p103)*.

Lumio
High up on the hillside on the opposite side of the gulf from Calvi, is the picturesque village of Lumio *(below)*, site of San Pietro, a Romanesque Pisan chapel founded in the 11th century.

Claim to Fame
Calvi's insistence that it, not Genoa, was the birthplace of Christopher Columbus rests on some shaky evidence: a family of weavers named "Colombu" did indeed live in the bastion while it served as a Genoese stronghold (Columbus' parents were definitely weavers). Additionally, the mariner named several New World settlements after Corsican saints. On the strength of such scraps the town has declared the great explorer as its mascot. Genoa, meanwhile, remains quiet on the subject.

Corte and its Hinterland

With its mildewing 18th-century buildings and spectacular mountain setting, Corte presents a very different aspect of the island from the Mediterranean chic prevailing on the coast. As the seat of Pascal Paoli's independent parliament, this was the crucible of Corsican nationalism. A strong sense of the island's cultural distinctiveness still pervades the streets here, especially during term time, when Corsican-speaking students crowd the café terraces. Close by, some awesome landscapes lie within easy reach – you can literally walk out of the centre and be in a complete wilderness within an hour.

Exterior of Oratoire St-Théophile

For a perfect picnic spot near the centre of Corte, head down the Avenue du Président Perucci and turn right just before the bridge to reach the riverside spot behind the Citadelle.

The patisserie Casanova, on the corner of Cours Paoli and Avenue Xavier Luciani, is a source of freshly baked local specialities.

- Map D6
- Tourist Office: www.corte-tourisme.com
- Musée de la Corse and Citadelle: Citadelle, Haute Ville; 04954 62670; 04954 52545; Open Apr–mid-Jun: 10am–6pm daily; mid-Jun–mid-Sep: 10am–8pm daily; mid-Sep–Oct: 10am–6pm Tue–Sun; Nov–Mar: 10am–5pm Tue–Sat; Adm €5.30; www.musee-corse.com
- Altipiani Outdoor Sports, 2 Place Paoli; 09603 70842; Adm €10; www.altipiani-corse.com

Top 10 Features

1. Cours Paoli
2. Treasure Hunt
3. Église de l'Annonciation
4. Oratoire St-Théophile
5. Place Gaffori
6. The Belvedere
7. Musée de la Corse
8. The Citadelle
9. Vallée du Tavignano
10. Vallée de la Restonica

Cours Paoli
Lined with lofty 18th-century buildings, Cours Paoli, Corte's main thoroughfare, is a legacy of its pivotal role in the Paoli era. It is full of shops, restaurants and bars; the cafés at the south end are the liveliest.

Treasure Hunt
Discover Corte's history and hidden architectural gems on a self-guided "treasure hunt" organized by the Altipiani agency. You'll need the help of locals to crack the clues.

Église de l'Annonciation
Joseph Bonaparte, Napoleon's elder brother, was christened in this mid-15th-century church *(left)* on Place Gaffori. One of the oldest buildings in Corte, this church's pride and joy is a wax statue of St Theophilus, the town's much loved patron saint.

4 Oratoire St-Théophile

The monk and freedom fighter Blaise de Signori, better known as St Theophilus, was the first and only Corsican to be canonized. He is honoured with this chapel sited near his birthplace in the Citadelle.

5 Place Gaffori

Walls still pock-marked by musket fire from the 1740s set the tone of this picturesque square in Corte's *haute ville* (upper town). A statue of independence hero, General Gaffori, points stridently skywards *(left)*.

7 Musée de la Corse

Housed in a building of glass and steel, Corte's cutting-edge museum showcases the island's traditional culture with exhibitions on farming, shepherding, religious brotherhoods *(above)*, tourism and music. Your ticket also gains you entry to the adjacent Citadelle.

9 Vallée du Tavignano

A wild, deep trench cutting from Corte to the fringes of the watershed, the Vallée du Tavignano shelters magnificent pine forests and enormous gorges. It can be accessed via a cobbled Genoese mule trail – a sublime walk.

6 The Belvedere

Clamber up a flight of ancient stone steps beneath the ramparts of the Citadelle to reach this popular vantage point, which offers panoramic views of the surrounding mountains.

8 The Citadelle

Perched on top of a near vertical crag, the town's Citadelle *(below)* is worth a visit for the views from its terraces over the crumbling *haute ville* and mountains.

A Nationalist Stronghold

Corte occupies a prominent position in the hearts and minds of local nationalists. It was here that Pascal Paoli convened his Assemblé Nationale, which founded the first Corsican-language printing press and drafted the Corsican constitution. Corte was also chosen as the site of the island's only university – a bastion of nationalism to this day.

10 Vallée de la Restonica

A road from Corte runs to this valley *(below)*. Jump on the shuttle bus in summer to reach Bergeries de Grotelle (shepherds' stone huts) and the lakes beyond.

Golfe de Porto

The combination of red porphyry and lapis-blue sea have made the Golfe de Porto Corsica's defining landscape. No other place in the Mediterranean boasts such a striking juxtaposition, which is all the more astonishing for its backdrop of high mountains. From May to September, visitors come in their thousands to marvel at the Calanche rocks, or to take boat trips to the Réserve Naturelle de Scandola. However, even at the height of summer it is possible to avoid the crowds by taking to the network of paved mule trails through the gulf's forested hinterland, or heading for the area's lesser known coves.

Exterior of Les Roches Rouges hotel

🚗 For a perfect car-free daytrip, take the boat to Girolata and walk up to the Col de la Croix *(see p74)* in time to catch the twice-daily bus back to Porto (summer only; check timings at any tourist office).

🍷 Sip a chilled Muscat on the terrace of Les Roches Rouges *(see p113)* in Piana, in the late afternoon when the views are lovely.

• Map A6
• Tourist Office: Porto marina; Map B6; 04952 61055; www.porto-tourisme.com • Porto Watchtower, Museum & Aquarium: Porto marina; Map B6; 04952 61924; Open Apr–Sep: 9am–7pm; Adm €6.50 • Boat Trips from Porto marina; Map B6; Porto Linea: 06081 68971, www.portolinea.com; Nave Va: 04952 18397, www.naveva.com • Piana Tourist Office: Place de la Mairie; 09669 28422; www.otpiana.com

Top 10 Features

1. Porto
2. Porto's Watchtower
3. Plage de Porto
4. Boat Trips
5. Calanche Walks
6. Piana
7. Capo d'Orto
8. Plage de Gradelle
9. The Corniche
10. Girolata

Porto
The scent of eucalyptus pervades Porto's harbour *(above)*, cowering beneath immense cliffs. It is an ideal base for forays around the bay.

Porto's Watchtower
Dwarfed by the escarpments around it, Porto's tower *(main image)* offers fine views out to the sea and up the valley. The aquarium next door is home to a rare lobster.

Plage de Porto
Broad, steeply shelving and covered in dusty grey pebbles, this is not the most inspiring beach in the area, but it does make for a highly scenic swim *(below)*.

4 Boat Trips
A flotilla of excursion launches leaves Porto marina daily in summer for tours of the gulf via its rock formations, sea caves and red cliffs, plus fishing trips.

5 Calanche Walks
The corniche wriggles through the centre of the world-famous rocks *(above)*, but to see the highlights, follow one of the waymarked trails outlined in leaflets on sale at the tourist offices in Porto and Piana.

6 Piana
Occupying a prime position on the island, Piana sits on a high natural balcony surveying the gulf. Stop at the Les Roches Rouges hotel *(see p113)* to sample the finest views in *fin-de-siècle* style.

7 Capo d'Orto
The region's ultimate viewpoint is the domed summit of a vast sugar-loaf mountain whose sheer north face looms above Porto *(above)*. A varied, easy-to-follow trail takes you to the top and back in around 5 hours.

8 Plage de Gradelle
Hardly anyone seems to know about this secluded pebble cove on the northern shore of the gulf, reached via a backroad off the main corniche. Magnificent views across the water are its chief attraction *(left)*.

9 The Corniche
This is Corsica's model coastal drive – though it can be a frustratingly stop-and-start experience in summer. Begin your journey in the early morning, when the light brings the red porphyry to life.

10 Girolata
The most picturesque village on the entire island, Girolata is nestled beneath the salmon-pink cliffs of Scandola. It can only be reached on foot from Col de la Croix *(above)*, or by boat from Porto.

Dragut in Girolata
Turgut Reis (1485–1565), a Greek-Ottoman privateer better known as "Dragut", was the scourge of the Mediterranean in the 16th century. In 1540, he and his fleet were caught by the Genoese in Girolata. Dragut remained in captivity for four years until his fellow corsair, Barabossa, forced his release, whereupon he promptly captured the town of Bonifacio.

Left **Battle of Ponte Nuovo** Right **Theodore von Neuhof**

Moments in History

1 1077: Corsica Becomes a Pisan Protectorate

To rein in the feuding local warlords who refused to swear allegiance to the Church, the Pope placed Corsica under Pisan "protection" – a state of affairs repeatedly challenged by rival Genoa. Some 300 Romanesque chapels survive on the island from the Pisan occupation.

2 1284: The Battle of Meloria

Genoa's naval victory over Pisa at the Battle of Meloria saw it wrest control of Corsica from its long-time adversaries. One of the most successful rebels of this era is the nobleman Sinucello della Rocca, nicknamed "Giudice" (the Judge), for his legendary sense of fairplay.

Genoese fleet at Meloria

3 1564: Sampiero Corso's Rebellion

Having gained a toe-hold on the island under an alliance with Henry II of France, the Corsican-born mercenary Sampiero Corso led a succession of uprisings against the Genoese, aided by the local lords. He died in a vendetta killing three years later at the hands of his wife's brothers.

4 1736: Theodore von Neuhof Uprising

This eight-month interlude, during which the German adventurer Theodore von Neuhof set himself up as "King of Corsica", ended after a couple of ineffectual sieges exposed his lack of military expertise and funds.

5 1754: Paoli Returns to Corsica

Son of an exiled nationalist hero, Pascal Paoli made a triumphant return to Corsica to spearhead a full-scale rebellion. Coins were minted, an elected assembly and printing press were set up in the new capital, Corte, and a liberal constitution was put in place. Meanwhile, Genoa ceded its territorial rights to France.

6 1769: The Battle of Ponte Nuovo

French forces slaughtered Paoli's ragtag army of patriots in a one-sided encounter on the Golo river. In its wake, resistance to French rule rapidly crumbled and Corsica became a fully integrated part of the French Republic, which it has remained ever since.

7 1918: The End of World War I

Corsica suffered terribly in the aftermath of World War I, with the highest per capita death rate

Preceding pages **The village of Aregno in the Balagne region** in any European region. With its work force decimated, the rural economy of the island's interior lapsed into a decline from which it has never recovered.

The armed Corsican resistance

1943: Liberation of Corsica
Hastened by the Allied invasion of southern Italy, Field Marshal Kesselring was forced to withdraw his Nazi forces from Corsica via Bastia. The Corsican resistance, or Maquis, fought the retreating Germans with great spirit, inspiring their counterparts on the mainland.

1975: The Siege of Aléria
A cell of Corsican nationalist paramilitaries took over the Depeille wine cellar near Aléria to protest against fraudulent wine-making practices by Algerian immigrants. In the ensuing shoot-out, two policemen died. The event marked the start of armed resistance against French rule.

1998: The Murder
Préfet Claude Érignac, the most senior French official in Corsica, was shot by a maverick nationalist gunman in Ajaccio. The atrocity galvanized attempts to resolve the armed conflict, which has left hundreds dead.

Top 10 Historical Figures

1 Sampiero Corso (1498–1567)
A flamboyant Corsican warlord, thought by some to have inspired Shakespeare's *Othello*.

2 Dragut (1485–1565)
One of the most feared pirates in history, Dragut was captured in Girolata.

3 Marthe Franchesini (1755–99)
Daughter of Corsican parents abducted by pirates in 1754, Marthe became the Queen of Morocco in 1786.

4 Theodore von Neuhof (1694–1756)
The much maligned "operetta king" from Westphalia, who ruled Corsica for eight months.

5 Gian Petro Gaffori (1704–53)
Corsican military commander who led the revolt against Genoese rule in the 1750s.

6 Pascal Paoli (1725–1807)
The founding father of independent Corsica.

7 Sir Gilbert Elliot (1751–1814)
Viceroy of Corsica during the Anglo-Corsican interlude of 1794.

8 Napoleon Bonaparte (1769–1821)
Born "Napoleone Buonaparte" in Ajaccio in 1769, the Emperor loathed the island of his birth.

9 Danielle Casanova (1909–43)
Corsican-born heroine of the French resistance, who died in Auschwitz.

10 Max (b. 1929) and Edmond Simeoni (b. 1934)
Masterminds of the Aléria siege of 1975, which kick-started the nationalist armed struggle in Corsica.

Left **Display at the Musée de l'Alta Rocca** Right **Dolmen de Fontanaccia**

🔟 Prehistoric Sites

1 Castellu d'Araggio
This marvellous Torréen site, high in the hills north of Porto-Vecchio, dates from 1500 BC and retains traces of prehistoric cooking fires. The views alone are worth a detour and there is a pleasant café serving refreshments, Orée du Site, next to the start of the path *(see p82)*.

2 Musée Départemental de Préhistoire Corse et d'Archéologie, Sartène
Drawn from all over Corsica, this collection of prehistoric artifacts is dominated by Neolithic pottery fragments, obsidian arrowheads and polished stone axes, but also includes pieces of gold jewellery and strings of coloured glass beads that look as fresh as the day they were buried *(see p14)*.

3 Filitosa
This privately owned site in southwest Corsica has earned UNESCO World Heritage status for its statue-menhirs, many of which sport skillfully carved faces and daggers – a trait of the island's Torréen population, who lived here nearly 4000 years ago. Don't miss visiting the small museum *(see pp12–13)*.

4 Site Archeologique de Cauria
Filitosa may be more famous, but two of the

carved menhirs at Stantari are the equal of their high-profile cousins in Valinco, with clearly sculpted features, diagonal swords and sockets in their heads into which horns must once have been fitted. The Dolmen de Fontanaccia and Alignements de Palaggiu and Rinaghju also lie in the same area *(see pp14–15)*.

5 Dolmen de Fontanaccia
This striking granite structure dates from the late-megalithic period when bodies, previously interred in stone coffins, were buried in stone chambers, which were themselves covered in compacted earth. The one at Fontanaccia, lost in the depths of the Sartenais region, ranks among the best preserved in southern Europe. Its former contents now reside in the museum at Sartène *(see p14)*.

6 Alignement de Palaggiu
Most of the 258 menhirs at this extraordinary site date from

Statue-menhirs of Filitosa

1800 BC. The grandfather of Corsican archaeology, Roger Grosjean, asserted they must have functioned as some kind of deterrent to would-be invaders because of their proximity to the coast. Whatever their origins, the stones still cast an undeniably eerie spell. To get to them, look for the turning just after the Mosconi vineyard on the left (see p15).

U Nativu

statue-menhir known as "U Nativu", dating from 900–800 BC. The statue bears distinct facial features and a T-shaped breastbone. Its sombre face has become something of a mascot for this famous wine-producing area. In August, it also enjoys pride of place at the village's guitar festival. ◈ Map E3

Pianu di Levie (Cucuruzzu)

A fairy-tale woodland of twisted oaks and mossy boulders enfolds the magical Pianu di Levie whose pièce de résistance, Cucuruzzu, is a well-preserved Torréen castle dating from around 1400 BC – complete with living chambers and slab roofs. A second site, Capula, lies a 20-minute walk away. All in all, this is a hugely atmospheric location which kids will adore (see p80).

Musée de l'Alta Rocca, Levie

This otherwise unremarkable village museum in Levie has a single prize exhibit: a human skeleton dating from 6570 BC known as "La Dame de Bonifacio" (a.k.a "La Dame d'Araguina"). The woman died in her mid-thirties and is thought to have been disabled by severely fractured legs, hence was in the care of her community. Also look out for the skeleton of the now extinct rabbit rat. ◈ Ave Lieutenant de Peretti, Quartier Pratu, Levie Map K4 • 04957 84634 • Open mid-Oct–Apr: 9am–noon, 1:30–5:15pm Tue–Sat; May–mid-Oct: 9am–6pm daily; Closed public hols • Adm • www.levie-altarocca.com

U Nativu, Patrimonio

In a shelter just south of Patrimonio church stands a superb

The Pieve Menhirs

It is well worth making the scenic trip to this little frequented village in the hills overlooking St-Florent to see its three statue-menhirs, which stand together on a terrace of raised ground next to the church. The family group, chiselled some 3,500 years ago from local granite, appear to be gazing wistfully over the valley – as well they might – the views are fabulous. ◈ Map E3

Left **St-Martin** Centre **Santa Maria Assunta** Right **Window in the apse, San Michele de Murato**

Churches and Cathedrals

1 La Canonica, Near Bastia

A hidden gem on Bastia's southern fringes, this elegant Romanesque cathedral was built by the Pisans in 1119 on the site of a 4th-century basilica. The Corinthian columns that decorate the church's exterior are believed to have originated from the Roman settlement that once stood opposite it *(see p19)*.

Relief on La Canonica

2 St-Jean-Baptiste, Bastia

With its gigantic twin belfries and solemn neoclassical façade, Corsica's largest church lends a typically Italian feel to the former Genoese harbour. The lavish rococo interior features gilt stucco, rare marble, trompe-l'oeil paintings and a papier-mâché statue of Christ resting on the high altar *(see p19)*.

St-Jean-Bapiste, Bastia

3 Oratoire de Monserato, Bastia

Cleanse yourself of all sins by ascending the Scala Santa in Bastia's famous Oratoire de Monserato. Only penitents willing to make the pilgrimage on their knees may approach the altar at the top of the staircase. A stepped ramp from opposite the main entrance, the 2-km (1-mile) long Chemin des Fillipines, leads to the Oratoire *(see p19)*.

4 Chapelle Ste-Christine, Cervione, Valle di Campoloro

The twin apses of this Romanesque chapel, nestled on a terrace overlooking the east coast near Cervione, retain late-15th-century frescoes, rendered in vibrant, earthy hues. Its patron, Saint Christina, is depicted next to a kneeling monk. The chapel, signposted off the D71, is a short way from Cervione on the left. ✆ *Map F6 • 04953 81140*

5 Santa Maria Assunta, St-Florent

Santa Maria Assunta ranks alongside La Canonica as the finest surviving Pisan edifice on the island. With enigmatic carvings of writhing serpents and wild animals, its arched entrance reveals a baroque interior whose chief possession is a glass coffin in which the mummified remains of Roman centurian St Flor are preserved *(see p22)*.

St-Martin, Patrimonio
6 Crowning the top of a wooded hillock, St-Martin is visible from all over Corsica's principal wine-growing region, many of whose growers feature the church on its labels. The bare brown schist campanile looks magnificent against the surrounding vineyards and chalk hills. Do not miss the famous limestone statue-menhir, "U Nativu", below it. ✆ Map E3

Nave, Oratoire de l'Immaculée Conception

San Michele de Murato
7 San Michele's trademark chequered pattern, rendered in grey-green serpentine and off-white marble, entices a steady stream of admirers. Dating from the 13th century, the church preserves a wealth of reliefs of peculiar carved beasts and human figures – typical of the Pisan period. It is also one of the few medieval shrines to have preserved its belfry. ✆ Map E4

St-Jean-Baptiste, Calvi
8 Founded in the 13th century, Calvi's honey-coloured cathedral had to be rebuilt after the Turkish siege of 1553, when its principal statue – Christ des Miracles – was brandished from the ramparts to repel the attackers. The statue now enjoys pride of place in a chapel to the right of the choir (see p25).

Oratoire de l'Immaculée Conception, Bastia
9 Dating from 1589, this lavishly decorated church has witnessed innumerable civic events in its time, including the initiation of the colonial governors. It was also where the British Viceroy, Sir Gilbert Elliot (see p33), once presided over the island's parliament. Velvet drapes and lashings of gold leaf give its interior the feel of an opera house (see p18).

Église de la Trinité et de San Giovanni, Aregno
10 This 12th-century Pisan masterpiece is built exactly like its contemporary San Michele de Murato, in a chequered pattern of green and cream blocks. Rising from the edge of Aregno, this church is encrusted with wonderful allegorical carvings of mythic beasts and folk figures. The most famous, crowning the apex, shows a man clasping his foot – thought to symbolize the "affliction of sin". ✆ Map C4

Left **Aiguilles de Bavella, near Zonza** Right **Music box created by artisans from Pigna**

🔟 Pretty Villages

Stairs leading to Sant'Antonino

Sant'Antonino, Balagne
Situated at the summit of a conical hill in the Balagne region of northwest Corsica, this village is the oldest inhabited settlement on the island. Its narrow vaulted alleyways and cobbled lanes have changed little since the Savelli lords ruled from here in the 9th century. ⊗ *Map C4*

Pigna
A very successful restoration project has resulted in the renovation of these formerly run-down medieval houses into a chocolate-box vision of neat stonework and blue-painted windows. The village has become a centre for traditional arts and crafts, with artisans beavering away in its workshops *(see p96)*.

Ota
Before Porto's development as a tourist hub *(see p28)*,

Ota was the gulf area's principal village, and remains a far more charming spot. The rear terraces of its bars enjoy superb vistas across to Capo d'Orto's cliffs *(see p29)*, while the Tra Mare e Monti Nord trail leads to some stunning viewpoints *(see p46)*.

Santa-Lucia-di-Mercurio
The best reason to drive out to Santa-Lucia-di-Mercurio, on the south side of the Vallée du Tavignano *(see p27)* in the Bozio region of central Corsica, is to admire it from a distance. Connoisseurs of great views will revel in the sight of its campanile and slate-roofed cottages set against the pale-grey crags and melting snow fields of distant Monte Rotondo. ⊗ *Map E6*

Ste-Lucie de Tallano
The orange-tiled rooftops of this Alta Rocca village *(see p12)*, spread over a high balcony looking across the Rizzanese Valley to the distant Sartenais coast, are a magical sight from higher up the mountain. The

Orange-tiled rooftops, Ste-Lucie de Tallano

village's 18th-century centre is ranged around a square where you can have wood-baked pizzas next to a fountain. ✎ Map K5

Montemaggiore
Montemaggiore straggles over a rocky ridge inland from Calvi, its ancient, buttressed-walled tower houses huddled around a church tower that is totally dwarfed by the intimidating bulk of Monte Grosso behind. For the best views, climb the outcrop at the eastern entrance to the village, known locally as "A Cima". ✎ Map C4

Évisa
Midway between the Golfe de Porto (see pp28–9) and Col de Verghio (see p72), the village of Évisa is swathed in chestnut forest. Paved mule paths dating from the Genoese era lead down woodland walks to secluded swimming spots, and the local restaurants excel in traditional mountain cuisine. ✎ Map B7

Morosaglia
This tiny village in the Castagniccia region is where Pascal Paoli (see p33) was born, and where his ashes are enshrined in a marble-lined chapel. From its fringes, where a couple of Romanesque churches hide in the maquis, chestnut forest gives way to a panorama of high ridges. ✎ Map E5

Zonza
One of the most clichéd images of the Corsican interior is that of Zonza, framed by the unmistakable Aiguilles de Bavella (Bavella needles). This village, where Muhammed V, Sultan of Morocco, was exiled in 1952, actually lies a long trek from the granite peaks, but it is

Zonza's main thoroughfare

no less picturesque for all that, especially after a rare dusting of Mediterranean snow. ✎ Map K4

Tralonca
Perched on the top of a conical hill on the opposite side of the valley from Corte, Tralonca lies about as far off the tourist trail as it is possible to get in Corsica. The village warrants a detour for its pretty core of square cottages, packed around a baroque church amid miles of terraced fields. ✎ Map D6

Left **Viewpoint on Capo Rosso** Right **Îles Sanguinaires**

Watchtowers and Lighthouses

View of the vineyards, Tour de Santa Maria

Tour de Santa Maria, Cap Corse

This tower is one of 91 structures erected by the Genoese in the 15th and 16th centuries as an early warning system against pirates. Cleft in half, Santa Maria cuts a forlorn figure at the far end of a bay of sparkling blue water, surrounded by vineyards, maquis and rolling hills. ◈ *Map E1*

Tour de Mortella, Désert des Agriates

Nelson was so impressed with the Tour de Mortella when he attacked it in 1794 that he copied its design for a chain of similar structures along the southern shores of Britain – the so-called "Martello Towers" *(see p23)*. Clearly visible from the excursion boats running to nearby Plage du Loto, it can only be reached on foot via the coast path. ◈ *Map E3*

Tour d'Agnello

Perched atop a high promontory on the north coast of Cap Corse, this tower provides a great vantage point from which to survey this particularly wild and beautiful stretch of coast. Come in spring when wild flowers carpet the surrounding clifftops. The path to it starts in Barcaggio village. ◈ *Map E1*

Tour de Capo Rosso

This spectacularly sited watchtower crowns a majestic red granite mountain at the southwest tip of the Golfe de Porto. Cliffs fall away to churning sea on three sides, while to the east a remarkable view unfolds over the bay to the high peaks inland. The trail starts 7 km (4 miles) west of Piana on the D84. ◈ *Map A7*

Tour de la Parata

The 12-m (39-ft) high Tour de la Parata dates from 1608. Its profile, rising from the top of a pyramidal headland at the northwestern tip of the Golfe d'Ajaccio, is echoed by

Tour de Mortella

that of the nearby Îles Sanguinaires (see p8), receding like stepping stones out to sea. The tower has its own tourist office and brand new *médiathèque* (multimedia library). ⊗ Map G3

Tour de Capo di Muro
Although less than an hour's drive from Ajaccio, Capo di Muro is as wild a promontory as any on the island. Locals wishing to get away from it all come here for a windy walk, heading down a rough path through the maquis to the tower crowning the headland's crest. ⊗ Map H4

Tour de Campomoro
The largest watchtower on the island, Tour de Campomoro presides over a picture-perfect bay, lined by a scattering of old fishermen's houses and hotels. Behind it, by contrast, lies a totally deserted shoreline where bleached granite boulders have been eroded into extraordinary shapes. The path continues all the way to Roccapina. ⊗ Map H5

Tour de Senetosa
Put on your hiking shoes and trek a couple of hours through dense juniper scrub and myrtle bushes to reach the magnificent Tour de Senetosa. Built of white granite, it sits astride a rocky ridge next to a wind-powered lighthouse, overlooking a string of remote beaches. Pick up the path to it in Tizzano, and take along plenty of water. ⊗ Map J6

Tour de Pinarellu
Rising from the crest of a low headland just north of Porto-Vecchio, this watchtower completes the perfect sweep of Pinarellu beach – a popular family hang-out in summer, and one where veterans of the infamous

Lighthouse at Capo Pertusato

GR20 mountain trail come to ease their aching feet (the path ends at nearby Conca). ⊗ Map L5

Phare de Pertusato
The most southerly spit of land in France, Capo Pertusato lies an hour's walk over the cliff tops from Bonifacio. Its lighthouse was constructed in 1838 to safeguard shipping in what still ranks among the most treacherous seaways in Europe. A stunning view over the Îles Lavezzi and Sardinia extends from the headland. ⊗ Map K7

Left **U Catenacciu** Right **Poster, Festival du Film du Lama**

Festivals

1 La Granitola, Calvi
Calvi's Easter festivities begin at 9pm on Good Friday when a procession of penitents carry wooden crosses through the *basse ville* (lower town) to the cathedral square up in the Citadelle. ✆ *Good Friday*

2 La Cerca, Erbalunga
This Easter procession by masked brotherhoods begins at the church of St-Erasme on the outskirts of Erbalunga in Cap Corse. ✆ *Good Friday*

3 U Catenacciu, Sartène
This procession of hooded penitents draws its participants from *confraternità* (local religious brotherhoods). Great secrecy surrounds the identity of the red-robed Pénitent Rouge – a role traditionally taken by repentant mafia godfathers. ✆ *Good Friday*

Open-air cinema, Lama

4 BD à Bastia
The centrepiece of Bastia's cartoon festival is an exhibition featuring an array of modern graphic art books, which range from time-honoured favourites such as TinTin and Asterix through to Marvel and Japanese anime. ✆ *04953 21281 • Late-Mar/early-Apr • www.una-volta.org*

5 Procession du Christ Noir, Bastia
The streets of Bastia's Citadelle form the backdrop for this religious procession, in which a black crucifix is paraded on the shoulders of devotees. The cross was discovered floating in the sea in 1428. ✆ *3 May*

6 Festival du Film du Lama
This niche film festival brings together film professionals from across Europe, and features movies inspired by rural themes. Screenings take place in an open-air cinema on the outskirts of Lama, whose bourgeois houses stand in striking contrast to the barren mountain slopes around it. ✆ *04954 82160 Late-Jul/early-Aug • www.festilama.org*

7 Rencontres Internationales de Théâtre en Corse, Olmi-Cappella, Pioggiola
For a week in August, this remote village in the Giunssani region transforms into the venue for a drama festival. Villagers perform plays on open-air stages and internationally famous directors help the participants prepare. ✆ *04956 19318 • Aug • www.ariacorse.org*

Fêtes Napoléoniennes, Ajaccio

Marching soldiers in First Empire uniform and sound and light extravaganzas bring a splash of pageantry to the Corsican capital in August, when the town celebrates the birthday of its most illustrious son. The grand finale, featuring an ear-splitting display of fireworks, is on Ascension Day (15 Aug).
✆ 04956 19318 • Mid-Aug

Fêtes Napoléoniennes, Ajaccio

International Festival du Cirque de Corse, Bastia and Ajaccio

Circus troupes from across the globe compete in this celebration for the young at heart, with exotic animals, jugglers, trainers and trapeze artists. ✆ Oct • www.imperialshow.com

Festival du Vent, Calvi

Calvi beach hosts this tourist season curtain closer, in which anything that can be flown on the end of a string is welcome to participate. Evenings feature lectures on environmental, wind-related subjects, and there are music recitals and concerts.
✆ 01532 09300 • Late-Oct • www.lefestivalduvent.com

Top 10 Country Fairs

Les Agrumes en Fete, Bastelicaccia

Exhibitors display citrus produce, with some recipes dating to the Court of Louis XV. ✆ Mar

Festa di L'Oliu Novu, Sainte Lucie de Tallano

Corsicans welcome the arrival of Spring by celebrating their hearty olive oil. ✆ Late-Mar–Apr

A Fiera di u Casgiu, Venaco

The island's largest cheese fest. The delicious smell of cheese permeates far and wide. ✆ May

Fiera di u Vinu, Luri

Sample Corsica's finest wines in an inspiring setting on Cap Corse. ✆ May

Fiera di San Petru, Lumio

Exhibition of stonemasonry and knife-making in a village overlooking Calvi. ✆ Jul

Foire de l'Olivier, Montemaggiore

Held in the Balagne mountains, this fair is dedicated to Corsican olive production.
✆ 04956 28172 • Jul

Foire de l'Amandier, Aregno

A fair to promote Corsica's ailing almond industry.
✆ 04956 97142 • Aug

Santa di u Niolo, Casamaccioli

Card games and traditional folk-singing wrap up this famous event in the Vallée de Niolo. ✆ Sep

Festa di u Ficu, Peri

A long-standing celebration of the regions' fig production and specialties. ✆ www.festadiuficu.com • Sep

Chestnut Festival, Bocognano

Showcases produce and recipes made from chestnut, with guided walks through woods. ✆ Dec

Left **A performance during Estivoce** Right **Crowds on the beach, Calvi on the Rocks**

Music Festivals

Calvi Jazz Festival

Calvi Jazz Festival
Popular jazz forms dominate the programme on Calvi's Quai Landry as the temperature starts to climb in late June. After gigs, performers let off steam with impromptu *boeufs* (jam sessions) in the waterfront bars. ⊗ *Late Jun • www.calvi-jazz-festival.com*

Estivoce, Balagne
Corsican vocal music – both polyphonic and instrumental – forms the backbone of this lively festival in Balagne. The larger events are staged in Pigna's modern, Moorish-style theatre. There are free sunset serenades every evening of the festival. ⊗ *Jul*

Calvi on the Rocks
This is not a big festival by international standards, but is great fun nonetheless. Bands and DJs play on open-air stages behind the beach. It is held at the height of the summer season. ⊗ *Jul • www.calviontherocks.com*

Le Nuits de la Guitare, Patrimonio
This guitar festival, held in the square below the village's church, has seen an impressive line-up of stars such as John McLaughlin, Elvis Costello, Gilberto Gil, Patty Smith and the great flamenco artist, Tomatito. Django-Reinhardt-style Gypsy Jazz tends to wrap up the event, which grows in stature each season. ⊗ *Jul • www.festival-guitare-patrimonio.com*

Porto Latino, St-Florent
For four nights in August, St-Florent's Place des Portes resounds to the infectious rhythms of salsa, mambo and Brazilian cumbia, as top-draw Latin dance groups take to the stage in this music festival. ⊗ *Mid-Aug • www.porto-latino.com*

Festival de Musique d'Erbalunga
A floodlit Genoese watchtower at the entrance to Erbalunga's tiny harbour provides a backdrop

Open-air stage, Calvi on the Rocks

for this high-season festival, held in the village's little square. French jazz and "le Rock" dominate the line-up, which spans the long weekend in mid-August. ✎ *Aug • www.festival-erbalunga.fr*

7 A Santa di u Niolu, Casamaccioli

A festival with ancient roots sees the bars in the mountain village of Casamaccioli overflow with aficionados of a dying Corsican art form – *chama i rispondi*. The performers improvise insults in rhyming couplets. ✎ *Vallée de Niolo • Sep*

8 U Settembrinu, Tavagna

This week-long event transforms the local squares into lively open-air stages in the Tavagna region. Rock, world music and folk are its mainstay with a strong showing from Corsican polyphony-fusion artists. ✎ *Eastern Corsica • Sep • www.tavagna.com*

9 Rencontres de Chants Polyphoniques, Calvi and Bastia

Corsica's most famous polyphonic choir, A Filetta, presides over this annual festival which attracts artists from all over the world. Mongolian throat singers, Bulgarian women's choirs and Georgian monks have all appeared in the past. ✎ *Mid-Sep*

10 Les Musicales de Bastia

Mostly French and Italian stars perform at Corsica's oldest and last big music festival of the year. Performances take place over five nights at different venues in Bastia, ranging from the Second Empire theatre to the Oratoire Ste-Croix. ✎ *Oct • www.musicales-de-bastia.com*

Top 10 Corsican Polyphony Albums

1 Intantu: A Filetta
The island's foremost group, famous for its traditional and contemporary polyphony.

2 Per Agata: Donnisulana
An all-women ensemble's first album that took the Corsican music world by storm.

3 Corsica Sacra: Jacky Micaelli
The finest female voice of her generation, Jacky is most expressive in this sparse, passionate recording.

4 A Bercy: I Muvrini
This is a platinum-selling live album of I Muvrini's performance at Bercy in Paris.

5 A Cappella: Tavagna
An old-school quintet from the island's eastern interior singing sublime polyphony.

6 Polyphonies: Voce di Corsica
A "supergroup" of Corsican singers formed in the 1990s. This album of polphony ranks as among the best ever.

7 L'Âme Corse: Various Artists
An album showcasing Corsica's polyphony output, with some instrumental tracks.

8 U Cantu di e Donne: Isulatine
A mixture of original compositions and traditional songs by an all-women group.

9 Isulanima: Trio Soledonna
Traditional musicians from around the Mediterranean team up with three of Corsica's finest female singers.

10 Poletti et le Choeur d'Hommes de Sartène
Traditional polyphony performed by the legend Jean-Paul Poletti and his male-voice choir group.

Left **Day walkers taking a break** Centre **Typical *gîte*** Right **Chestnuts in forest, Évisa–Ota trail**

Treks and Walks

1 GR20
Corsica's legendary high-altitude trek, tackled by around 18,000 people each year, ranks among the most challenging multi-stage itineraries in Europe. It is a tough 10-day adventure not to be undertaken lightly. ✎ *Map C5*

2 Tra Mare e Monti Nord
This is Corsica's second-most popular walking route after the GR20 and takes you through the red-granite landscapes of the northwest. The village of Girolata, with its beaches and mountainous hinterland, is the route's highlight *(see p29)*. ✎ *Map B4*

3 Mare a Mare Nord
A classic coast-to-coast route, this trail winds across the island at its widest point, via a

Mare a Mare Nord trail

parade of scenic highlights, including the Gorges du Tavignano and Vallée de Niolo *(see p86)*. This is among the lesser visited long-distance paths. ✎ *Map G1*

4 Mare a Mare Sud
A five-day traverse of the idyllic far south of the island, this trail is punctuated by *gîtes d'étapes* (lodges) where you can unwind at the end of every stage. Landscapes vary from pristine oak forest to grassy uplands, with many swimming spots along the way. ✎ *Map J5*

5 Campomorro–Roccapina
A terrific two-day coastal hike along the rugged shoreline of the Sartenais *(see pp14–15)*, this route is peppered with beautiful coves and watchtowers. However, navigation can be tricky and there is very little shade or water along the route. ✎ *Map H5*

6 Sentier des Douaniers, Cap Corse
A two-day coastal itinerary around the wild northern tip of Cap Corse *(see pp20–21)*, this trail takes in turquoise bays and scrubland. Starting at Macinaggio, it winds to Centuri-Port, via an overnight stop at Barcaggio. ✎ *Map F1*

7 Sentier Littoral, Désert des Agriates
Three days are generally advised for this wild coastal hike along the edge of the Désert des Agriates *(see p23)*. There is a

camp site at Saleccia and a refuge at Plage de Guigno, but there are no other facilities. In early summer you'll have the stunning beaches all to yourself. ◈ *Map D3*

8 Évisa–Ota

This is a popular half-day walk through the fragrant chestnut forest that separates two of the island's prettiest hill villages. Tackle the paved Genoese mule track uphill from Ota or start in Évisa. At the midway point, the Pont de Zaglia spans a gorgeous picnic and swimming spot. ◈ *Map B7*

Lac de Capitello

9 Lacs de Melo et Capitello

The path up the grandiose Restonica valley to this pair of exquisite glacial lakes gets jammed with hikers in high summer, but follow it in May or September and you are in for a treat. The reward is a vast amphitheatre of rock, scree and snow surrounding two shimmering blue lakes, formed at different altitudes. ◈ *Map K1*

10 Trou de la Bombe

This family-friendly amble takes you through the soaring granite pinnacles and pine forests of Bavella en route to the famous *Trou* – a large hole, created by wind erosion in a vast escarpment. Climb up for dizzying views down to the coast. ◈ *Map L4*

Top 10 Trekking Tips

1 Wild Camping
It is illegal to wild camp in Corsica, so plan your accommodation in advance.

2 Booking Gîtes
Beds in lodges should always be booked well ahead. Full board is generally obligatory.

3 Refuges
Refuge places are allocated on a first-come-first-served basis. Camping and bivouacking are permitted around the huts.

4 Waymarks
Do not venture away from the waymarks unless you have the navigation skills to find them again.

5 Water
Always check with the locals about water sources, and take along a spare bottle in case you run out.

6 Sun
Underestimate the power of the Corsican sun at your peril. Sunstroke at an altitude can be lethal.

7 Guide Books
The Féderation Française de la Randonnée Pédestre (FFRP) publishes excellent guides for all Corsica's long-distance routes.

8 Hygiene
Dispose of toilet paper responsibly; do not leave it on the trails.

9 Trekking Poles
Carry a pair of adjustable trekking poles to ease the knee strain on long ascents and descents.

10 Fuel
If you plan to cook, take a multi-fuel stove as not all makes of gas canister are available in Corsica.

Left **Boat to Plage du Loto** Right **Plage de Saleccia**

🔟 Great Beaches

Plage de Palombaggia
Palombaggia's trio of gently shelving bays, lapped by shallow, turquoise water, are perfect for children. A row of stately umbrella pines provides shade in the dunes behind and there is a terrific beach café at the southernmost cove – Le Tamaricciu *(see p83)* – serving gourmet snacks and cold chestnut beer. Jump on the bus from Porto-Vecchio (summer only) to get here. ✆ *Map L6*

Plage de Saleccia
It is probably impossible to identify the clearest waters in Corsica, but those off Saleccia must be in contention. Low rainfall in this desert area ensures minimal runoff from streams, leaving the shallows crystalline – perfect for snorkelling. The beach is as far-flung as it is beautiful. Camp in the site behind to enjoy seeing the sand turn red at sunrise and sunset. ✆ *Map D3*

Santa Giulia
If it weren't for the Corsican maquis and Mediterranean villas spread over the surrounding hills, this bay of dazzling aquamarine water and soft white sand could be mistaken for the Caribbean. The beach gets jam-packed in the school holidays, as it lies within an easy drive of Porto-Vecchio, as well as some of the island's camp sites. ✆ *Map L6*

Plage de Roccapina
Water as transparent and sand as soft as anywhere in the Mediterranean are overlooked by a lion-shaped rock formation and watchtower here. Access to this beach is via a badly rutted track, which keeps the crowds at arm's length. Climb the path up the headland to the north for a bird's eye view of the cove. ✆ *Map J6*

Plage de l'Ostriconi
Only a handful of visitors pull off the highway between Bastia and Calvi to enjoy this

Plage de l'Ostriconi

unspoilt, deserted bay. Facilities are nonexistent, though wood chalets and camping space are available a little way inland. ⚲ Map C3

Plage de Rondinara
A clam-shaped lagoon entered via a slim gap between two headlands, this isolated bay between Porto-Vecchio and Bonifacio does not attract the crowds you'd expect given how lovely it is – except in peak season, when the camp site behind it fills up. Bring your snorkelling kit, as the underwater life is prolific. A lively beach café supplies the essentials. ⚲ Map L6

Plage de Petit Sperone
This hidden gem is tucked away at the southeastern-most tip of the island, below a complex of millionaires' retreats and an exclusive golf course. It is not even marked on IGN maps, but you can reach the cove via a footpath from the beach at Piantarella nearby, where there is a rough lay-by to park in. ⚲ Map K7

Plage de Cupabia
Discover this glorious bay at the far northeastern end of the Golfe de Valinco. The sea can get choppy here if there is a strong westerly wind blowing, but in calm weather the shallows are fine for kids to swim in. Facilities extend to a small café, car park and basic camp site. ⚲ Map H4

Plage d'Erbaju
Climb over the headland north of Roccapina and follow the track downhill to a spectacular 2-km (1-mile) sweep of coarse sand, where you are guaranteed lots of space even at the height of summer. The chic

Stone huts at the Murtoli estate

Murtoli estate's rental cottages *(see p111)* are the only buildings visible for miles. ⚲ Map J6

Plage du Loto
Catch a boat from St-Florent to reach this splendid beach with shining white sand and turquoise sea water, tucked away on the Désert des Agriates' pristine, rocky coast. The views across the gulf to the mountains of Cap Corse are unforgettable. ⚲ Map E3

Left **Genoese bridge, Pont de Muricciolu** Right **Cascade des Anglais**

🔟 Wild Swims

Plage de Guignu
A five- to six-hour walk from the nearest road on the Désert des Agriates coastal path brings you to this magical cove. With total wilderness on all sides, its turquoise waters lie beyond the reach of all but the most determined trekkers. The Refuge de Ghuignu provides basic accommodation. 🔊 Map D3

Cala di Tuara
After an hour's hot hike through the maquis dividing Girolata from the Col de la Croix (see p74), Cala di Tuara is a welcome sight. Few can resist the lure of its amazingly clear water, shimmering blue above a bed of grey granite pebbles. The

Cala di Tuara

cove also shelves quickly and offers some terrific deep-water snorkelling. 🔊 Map A6

Cala Genovese and Cala Francese
This pair of isolated coves is the jewel of Cap Corse's northern shoreline. Piles of seaweed sometimes mask their soft white sand, but the water is clear and the shallows are ideal for any children in your party – though you'll probably have to carry them most of the way from Macinaggio (see p20). 🔊 Map F1

Tuarelli
On the edge of this far-flung hamlet in Corsica's rugged northwest, the Fango river drains through smoothed boulders that shelter perfect natural pools to swim in when water levels are low during the summer. A huge wall of blood-red mountains – the "Grande Barrière" of Paglia Orba's north face – forms an enthralling backdrop. 🔊 Map B6

Lonca
Although a bit crowded at the height of summer, this old-favourite bathing place in the secluded Lonca Valley deserves a detour from the nearby D124. Deep green pools froth with water surging over granite slabs, shaded beneath a canopy of Mediterranean oak and chestnut forest. The site lies an easy five-minute walk from the road. 🔊 Map B6

6 Piscines Naturelles d'Aïtone

This classic picnic spot is nestled under vast Laricio pine trees just below the Col de Verghio (see p72). The roar of the falls is as invigorating as the deep pools they flow into and there are river-smoothed granite boulders to sprawl on after taking a dip. ✎ Map C6

Piscines Naturelles d'Aïtone

7 Cascade des Anglais

In the early 20th century, these beautiful waterfalls, high on the watershed near the railway station in Vizzavona, used to attract daytripping English aristocrats from Ajaccio – whence their name. Nowadays they are firmly on the tourist trail, thanks to the exquisite pine forest and grandiose mountain scenery on all sides. Call in for a coffee at the delightfully old-fashioned Hotel Monte d'Oro. ✎ Map K1

8 Pont de Muricciolu, Albertacce

This heavenly bathing spot, high in the Vallée de Niolo beside another secluded old Genoese bridge, is generally the exclusive preserve of hikers following the Mare a Mare Nord path (see p46). You can walk to it in about 20 minutes from the D84 – look for the trail peeling north just after the crucifix on the outskirts of Albertacce village. ✎ Map C6

9 Plage d'Argent

Appreciate the silver sand and turquoise water of the Sartenais coast in solitude at this remote cove. You can reach here after half-an-hour's drive down a rutted track, opposite the turning for the Palaggiu menhirs (see p15), followed by another half hour's trek over the gravelly sand of Plage de Tralicetu. ✎ Map J6

10 Pont Génois, Asco

A humpbacked, 16th-century Genoese bridge spans the stretch where the normally turbulent Asco river flows calm and deep. Bring a face mask to see the trout that lurk in the river's cold, green depths, and a pair of hiking shoes to explore the ancient path continuing up the mountain. Asco village lies 22 km (14 miles) west of Ponte Leccia on the D147. ✎ Map D5

Left **The white cliffs of Bonifacio** Right **Kiosk selling tickets for boat trips to Plage du Loto**

Boat Trips

Boat trip from Ajaccio to Capo d'Orto

Golfe d'Ajaccio
Ajaccio looks dazzling when viewed from the bay. Boats leave Port Tino Rossi daily in summer for trips along the Rive Sud to Capo di Muro *(see p74)*, with a stop for coffee and a swim en route. ⊗ *Nave Va, Port Tino Rossi, Ajaccio • Map H3 • 04952 18397 • www.naveva.com*

Îles Lavezzi
The Îles Lavezzi are a cluster of low-lying islets in the Straits of Bonifacio *(see p79)*. Boats shuttle to and from them throughout the day, leaving you ample time to snorkel amid some of the Mediterranean's most colourful marine life. ⊗ *Marine de Bonifacio • Map L7 • 04951 09750*

Santa Teresa di Gallura
The ferry ride from Bonifacio to Santa Teresa di Gallura in the north of Sardinia is thrilling, affording superb views of the fabled white cliffs of Bonifacio. ⊗ *Map K7 • www.mobylines.com, www.saremar.it*

Îles Cerbicale
The highlight of boat trips from Porto-Vecchio's harbour are the Îles Cerbicale, an archipelago of islets rising from the turquoise waters off Plage de Palombaggia *(see p81)*. Longer excursions continue on to Bonifacio and Îles Lavezzi, stopping for a dip at a secluded cove on the return leg. ⊗ *Chiocca Croisières, Porto Vecchio harbour • Map L5 • 04957 14150 • www.amour-des-iles.com*

Sea Kayaking, Aléria
Kayaks can be rented from the Club Nautique d'Aléria. The firm organizes kayak lessons, guided hikes and offers river expeditions on the Tavignano river. ⊗ *Map M1 • 06380 24530 • www.cnaleria.blogspot.fr*

Cap Corse
Jump aboard the *San Paulu* in Macinaggio marina for a jaunt along the beautiful north coast of Cap Corse. The boat anchors for lunch at Barcaggio village, where there is a particularly pleasant little café-restaurant *(see p99)*. ⊗ *San Paulu, Port de Plaisance, Macinaggio harbour • Map F1 • 04953 50709 • www.sanpaulu.com*

Plage du Loto
You'll never forget the first time you set eyes on beautiful Plage du Loto. A rolling ride across the gulf from St-Florent, the cove's brilliant turquoise waters remain hidden until you

are almost upon them. Depart early and you'll have time to walk to Salecccia. ✎ *Le Popeye, Campo d'Elge, St-Florent • Map E3 • 04953 71907 • www.lepopeye.com*

Golfe de Porto
Colombo Line takes you from Calvi's Quai Landry (see p24) around the northwest coast to the Réserve Naturelle de Scandola and Calanche in the Golfe de Porto (see p28–9). The launches stop at Girolata for a scenic lunch overlooking the beach. ✎ *Colombo Line • Map A6 • 04956 53210 • www.colombo-line.com*

Girolata and Réserve Naturelle de Scandola
A fleet of excursion boats chugs out of Porto's marina during the summer, shuttling visitors out to the famous Réserve Naturelle de Scandola, with its soaring red cliffs. Boats stop for lunch at Girolata. ✎ *Via Mare, Porto marina • Map A6 • 06072 87272 • www.viamare-promenades.com*

The village of Girolata

Calanche de Piana
The hidden sea caves and volcanic rocks of the Calanche (see p29) feature on boat tours of the Golfe de Porto's southern shore. Boats run from Porto as far as the foot of Capo Rosso, while full-day sailings cross the bay to Scandola and Girolata (see p29). ✎ *Porto Linea • Map B7 • 04951 04924, 06081 68971 • www.portolinea.com*

Top 10 Dive Sites

Mérouville, Bouches de Bonifacio
Large colonies of grouper are the biggest draw of this celebrated dive site. ✎ *Map K7*

Les Cathédrales et les Aiguilles, Golfe de Valinco
These spectacular underwater mountain ranges of peaks fissures and rock arches, are inhabited by 60 species of fish. ✎ *Map J5*

Le Tonneau and Red Canyon, Golfe de Valinco
There are exceptional diving opportunities at this pair of deep-water sites. ✎ *Map J5*

Capo di Muro, Ajaccio
The most southerly point in the gulf has abundant sea life. ✎ *Map H4*

Le Banc Provençal, Golfe de Lava
An Aladin's Cave of rainbow wrasse and multi-coloured sea sponges. ✎ *Map G2*

Vardiola and Punta Mucchilina, Golfe de Porto
Coral is abundant at these two benchmark sites. ✎ *Map A6*

L'Ila Morsetta, Galéria
This giant underwater boulder choke teems with conger eels and lobster. ✎ *Map B5*

B-17, Calvi
Shot down in 1944, this American bomber rests in the turquoise water. ✎ *Map B4*

Pain de Sucre and la Canonnière, Bastia
These impressive rock formations lurk in the seas just north of Bastia. ✎ *Map F3*

Le Danger du Toro, Porto-Vecchio
Cliffs plunge to 40 m (131 ft) where you can see red coral, grouper and an impressive canyon. ✎ *Map L5*

Left **L'Oriu de Cani** Centre **Aiguilles de Bavella** Right **Grouper, Bouches de Bonifacio**

ᴛᴏᴘ10 Natural Wonders

Laricio pines, Forêt d'Aïtone

1 Laricio Pines, Forêt d'Aïtone

Some venerable old Laricio pines surviving in the island's high forests, such as Aïtone below the Col de Verghio, reach a height of 40 m (131 ft), making them the tallest conifers in Europe. The Genoese used to prize the trees as ships' masts but they are now protected (see p72).

2 Paglia Orba

Soaring above the Vallée de Niolo (see p86), Paglia Orba, at 2525 m (8284 ft), is one of Corsica's highest mountains and a most distinctive peak, owing to its shark's-fin shape. The ascent – a two-hour scramble from Ciottulu a i Mori refuge (see p90) – is simpler than it looks from below. ⊗ Map C6

3 Lac de Nino

Wild horses graze the green pastures surrounding this divine high-altitude lake. A long, uphill walk is required to get here but the effort is rewarded with the very first glimpse of the glass-like water, its surface reflecting the backdrop of snow-streaked peaks and ridges (see p89).

4 Spelunca Gorge

Awesome cliffs flank this deep valley, which snakes inland from Porto to the Col de Verghio pass into the Niolo region. Natural pools in the river at its base offer plenty of swimming spots from where you can admire the scenery (see p71).

5 The White Cliffs of Bonifacio

Plenty of seagulls swarm above Bonifacio's corrugated chalk escarpments. The cliffs are so eroded at their base that they seem on the verge of collapse – which they have done in places, as shown by chunks of fallen

Chalk escarpments of Bonifacio

debris. See them at their most striking on a boat trip out of the harbour. ⊚ *Map K7*

Calanche de Piana

The contorted, eroded orange granite of the Calanches de Piana covers the mountainside into the Golfe de Porto *(see pp28–9)*. The corniche cuts right through the middle of the Calanche, giving access to a network of way-marked trails. Some of the strangest rock formations can be seen on a boat trip from Porto.

Aiguilles de Bavella

A phalanx of seven mighty pinnacles crumbling into a carpet of pine forest, the needle-shaped peaks of Bavella look like a vision from some fantasy novel. Whether viewed up close from the waymarked scrambling routes around their bases, or from the white Madonna statue at the Col, the needles present a breathtaking spectacle *(see p80)*.

L'Oriu de Cani

Shaped like a witch's hat, this rock, rising above the tiny hamlet of Cani, is associated with all manner of spooky tales. Children will love its enigmatic appearance when the shadows lengthen in late afternoon. Cani lies 20 km (12 miles) southwest of Porto-Vecchio, near the village of Chera on the D59. ⊚ *Map K6*

Grouper

Slow-moving and faintly comical with their prominent lips, grouper *(mérou)* are the stars of the Corsican underwater world. Divers literally queue up in the Bouches de Bonifacio to visit one colony whose members have become tame enough to touch *(see p53)*.

Sea caves, Scandola

Scandola

Accessible only by sea, the terracotta headland at the northwest entrance to the Golfe de Porto is the most heavily protected land in France – a precious wild habitat and spectacular geological oddity. Experience the magical sea caves, giant eagles' nests and porphyry rock formations around its fringes on a boat excursion out of Porto's marina *(see p53)*.

Left **Kayakers on a rushing torrent** Right **Capo d'Orto, popular for rock climbing**

TOP 10 Outdoor Activities

1 Hiking
Take to the network of long-distance hiking trails to explore Corsica's rugged interior. Ranging from two-day coastal ambles to the two-week marathon of the GR20 *(see p46)*, the routes are all well equipped with hostels and huts. ↔ www.parc-corse.org

2 Canyoning
This adventure sport, which allows you to climb and abseil through stream gorges using ropes and harnesses, has caught on fast in Corsica. The island's side valleys offer many possibilities for outfits running guided trips. ↔ www.corse-montagne.com

3 Mountain Biking
The tracks winding through Corsica's magnificent forests and along the more open stretches

Mountain biking along Bonifacio's cliffs

of coast make for some superb rides. One of the most popular off-road adventures is the 11-km (7-mile) cycle through the Désert des Agriates to Saleccia *(see p23)*. ↔ www.vttencorse.fr

4 Kayaking
Beach hop along the wilder stretches of Corsica's coastline by rented kayak. Organized expeditions involve bivouacs in deserted coves and circumnavigating promontories such as Scandola and Capo Rosso. Beginners can start on the shoreline off Aléria, where a local firm offers tuition *(see p52)*. ↔ www.corsekayak.com

5 Via Ferrata
Winding up spectacular rock faces and ridges, via ferratas enable climbers to navigate mountain routes without needing to use their own ropes. ↔ www.viaferrata.org

6 Adventure Parks
A big craze in Corsica are adventure parks, where areas of forest have been equipped with cable bridges, aerial walkways and zip slides to create courses that get your pulse racing *(see p58)*.

7 Snorkelling and Diving
Corsica's underwater topography is no less spectacular than the terrain on dry land, with sudden drops from sandy bottomed bays to blue

voids nearly 1000 m (3300 ft) deep in some places. Multi-coloured fish are a common sight while snorkelling, and dive prospects rank among the most exciting in Europe. ✎ www.plonger-en-corse.com

Diver looking at marine life

Rock Climbing
Corsica boasts a number of rock climbing hot spots. The most famous of them are the Aiguilles de Bavella in the south, the red escarpments crenellating Paglia Orba *(see p54)* and the awe-inspiring north face of Capo d'Orto near Porto on the west coast *(see p29)*. ✎ www.escalade.corse.topo.free.fr

Horse Riding
Riding a horse over a white sand beach and bathing the animal afterwards in transparent sea water is an experience few places in the world can offer. Bred to thrive in Corsica's rough terrain, local ponies await riders at a dozen or more equestrian centres dotted around the island. ✎ www.randonee-equestre-corse.com

Skiing
Corsica is not exactly known as a winter sports destination. However, if you happen to be on the island after a rare blizzard, join the exodus to the three surviving ski stations at E'Capannelle (Ghisoni), Val d'Ese (northeast of Ajaccio) and Verghio (Niolo). ✎ www.ffski-corse.com

Top 10 Ultimate Views

Monte Cinto
On a clear day, you can see the distant Alps from Corsica's highest summit at 2706 m (8900 ft). ✎ *Map C6*

Monte Corona
An astounding panorama of the watershed peaks unfolds from this mountain top above Calenzana. ✎ *Map C5*

Notre-Dame-de-la-Serra
The views over the Golfe de Calvi from this hilltop chapel are magnificent. ✎ *Map B4*

Capo d'Orto
This domed peak provides a great vantage point over the Golfe de Porto. ✎ *Map B7*

Capo Rosso
Climb this tower-topped headland for a staggering vista over the Calanches and gulf to Paglia Orba. ✎ *Map A7*

Chemin des Crêtes
There are superb views over the capital and its gulf, from this high path. ✎ *Map H3*

Tour de Roccapina
This tower overlooks a paradise cove on one side and a vast empty beach of white sand on the other. ✎ *Map J6*

Capo Pertusato
The culminating point of Bonifacio's white cliffs reveal a terrific view across the straits to Sardinia. ✎ *Map K7*

Foca Alta, Cartalavonu
This high pass in the Massif de l'Ospédale above Porto-Vecchio *(see p81)*, overlooks the turquoise southwest coast. ✎ *Map K5*

Monte San Petrone
Ascend Corsica's holy summit for a 360-degree panorama over the chestnut forests of Castagniccia *(see p87)*. ✎ *Map E6*

Left **Plage de Pinarello** Centre **Tramway train, L'Île Rousse** Right **Corsica Madness adventure park**

🔟 Children's Attractions

1 Donkey Rides

With its sea views, olive groves and shady paths, the bucolic countryside of the Baracci Valley, inland from Propriano, is perfect for sedate rambles on donkey back. Ride through lovely oak forests via ancient paved mule tracks to the mountain villages overlooking the valley. ✎ *Asinu di Campitellu, Route du Maggiese, Figuccia, near Propriano • Map J4 • 06032 88185 • Open Apr–Sep*

2 A Cupulatta

More than 3,000 animals and 170 species of tortoises, turtles and terrapins are represented at this reptile breeding and research centre. Kids are encouraged to handle a few of them, and there are usually some cute newborns to amuse visiting tots *(see p72)*.

Galapagos tortoise at A Cupulatta

3 Village des Tortues de Moltifao

With Corsican tortoises becoming increasingly rare due to habitat destruction, the focus in this sanctuary, run by the National Park authority, is on breeding endemic species for release into the wild. ✎ *Route d'Asco, Tizzarella, Moltifao • Map D5 • 04954 78503 • Open May–Sep by appt for guided visits only • Adm • www.parc-corse.org*

4 Corsica Madness Adventure Park

This sprawling adventure park, in a Laricio pine forest just below the Aiguilles de Bavella, occupies a most spectacular site. Choose between three circuits featuring monkey bridges, vertical nets and 110-metre zip slides – all against wonderful mountain views. ✎ *Bavella • Map L4 • Open May–Oct: 9:30am–6:30pm • Adm • www.corsicamadness.com*

5 A Tyroliana

A short drive inland from the coast around Porto-Vecchio, this riverside adventure park offers a mix of vertigo-inducing thrills in a shady pine forest, with pleasant picnic spots and river swimming nearby. ✎ *Route de Taglio Rosso, Poggio del Pino 20144, Ste-Lucie-de-Porto-Vecchio • Map L4 • 06184 04439 • Open Mid-Apr–end-May: afternoons; Jul & Aug: 10am–7pm • Adm • www.atyroliana.com*

6 Tramway de Balagne

Corsica's train line across the mountains is undoubtedly one of the great experiences the island has to offer. However, the journey can be a little too long for children. One compromise is to jump on the orange-and-yellow tramway train shuttling between L'Île Rousse and Calvi, which skirts some of the northwest's finest beaches, stopping at 20 stations en route. ● *Map C4 • 04956 50091 • Four to six departures daily • www.ter-sncf.com*

Corsica Forest

Just inland from Solenzara, Corsica Forest consists of a very well-equipped adventure park and a challenging via ferrata facility installed around a massive cliff overlooking a bend in the river. As ever, a head for heights is needed. Canyoning is an optional add-on. ● *On the D268 near Solenzara • Map L3 • 06161 80058 • Open Jun–Sep: 9am–6pm • Adm • www.corsica-forest.com*

Tri-yaking

Rent a tri-yak – just like a kayak, only with places for two adults and a child – for a paddle around the exquisite Pinarello bay and its adjacent island – a good place for beginners of sea canoeing. ● *Sport-sica, Plage de Pinarello, Ste-Lucie-de-Porto-Vecchio • Map L5 • 06242 65183 • Mid-Apr–mid-Oct*

Jardin des Abeilles

Corsican honey is out of this world – especially the variety made from maquis or chestnut flower pollen. Tours of this little bee garden just outside Ajaccio will introduce children to the honey-making process, with glimpses into a glass-sided hive and demonstrations of extraction techniques. Tasting sessions are also held. ● *Chez Denis Casalta, Ocana 20117 • Map K2 • 04952 38388 • Open Jun–mid-Sep 9am–6:30pm Mon–Fri, 10am–6:30pm Sat–Sun; mid-Oct–Mar group tours only; Boutique open all year • www.lesjardindesabeilles.com*

Visitor with animals, Parc Naturel d'Olva

Parc Naturel d'Olva

Animal-loving children can mingle with a menagerie of donkeys, goats, ponies, ducks, chickens and peacocks at this small holding in the beautiful Rizzanese Valley, just below Sartène. The farmers also lay on nature walks and goat-milking demonstrations, and there's a picnic area. ● *Route de la Castagna, Sartène • Map J5 • 06117 52964 • Open Apr–May & Oct: 10am–6pm Tue–Sun; Jun–Sep: 9:30am–7pm daily; Nov –Mar: 10am–6pm Wed, Sat–Sun & school hols • Adm • www.parc-animalier-corse.com*

Left **Local meat shop displaying meats & sausages** Right **Wild boar & veal terrine**

TOP 10 Culinary Specialities

1 Charcuterie
The diet of Corsica's free-range pigs – windfallen chestnuts, roots and wild berries – is the secret behind the island's aromatic cured meats. They come in a variety of forms: *prisutu* (ham); *lonzu* (fillet); *figatellu* (strong liver sausage); *coppa* (shoulder); *valetta* (cheek) and *salamu* (spicy salami).

2 Brocciu
Brocciu (pronounced "broodge") is soft ewe's cheese, produced uniquely in the winter, which Corsicans love for the full flavour and creamy texture it lends to many dishes. It blends wonderfully well with mint to make the filling for cannelloni, and the stuffing for Bonifacio's traditional baked aubergine.

3 Sanglier (Wild Boar)
Despite the annual onslaught from hunters in the winter, wild boar remain prolific in the forests of the Corsican interior. If you're lucky enough to be here during hunting season you'll find local menus dominated by wild pork stews and fillets, grilled with maquis herbs in smokey open hearths.

4 Veal and Olives
This classic Corsican dish features on the menus of most Corsican restaurants all year round. Like the pigs, local calves tend to be grazed in the maquis, where they feed on unfertilized woodland and mountain pastures, ensuring a fuller flavour which is perfectly complimented by strong Alta Rocca olives.

5 Miel de Châtaigne (Chestnut Flower Honey)
If you like your honey strong and packed with exotic aromas, pick up a pot of *miel de châtaigne* at a local deli and prepare yourself for a taste of heaven. Chestnut-flour biscuits provide the ideal accompaniment.

6 Tianu (Game Stew)
Corsicans are passionate hunters and will shoot anything that flutters in the maquis. Most of the small game ends up in hearty *tianu* (stew), typically made with *bécasse* (woodcock), *pédrix* (partridge), *caille* (quail) and any unlucky songbird that strays into the riflemen's sights.

7 Beignets (Fritters)
Light and nutty, chestnut-flour beignets are a perennial Corsican favourite, often served

Beignets

as a starter. The best of them are made with brocciu. Beignets frequently appear wrongly translated on local menus as "doughnuts", a description that does not do them justice.

Fromage de Brébis (Ewe's Cheese)

Pungent and filled with mountain flavours, Corsican matured ewe's cheese derives its intensity from the herb-filled pastures the sheep graze on during the summer, and the cheese-making techniques used by shepherds, which have altered little over the ages.

Potato pie made with ewe's cheese

Pâté de Merle (Blackbird Pâté)

If you are wondering why there aren't more songbirds hopping around Corsican lawns, the answer is the local penchant for pâtés, particularly those made from *merles* (blackbirds) – still highly prized by the islanders despite objections from bird-lovers on the French mainland.

Chestnuts

The Genoese planted whole forests of chestnut trees on the island, and the flour derived from the dried nuts is still an essential ingredient in many traditional dishes, particularly those of the mountains. Most patisseries in Corsica serve a range of cakes and pastries and even bread, made with chestnut flour.

Top 10 Markets and Delis

1 Farmers' Market, Ajaccio
A huge selection of locally produced charcuterie, cheese and wine (see p9).

2 U Stazzu, Ajaccio
The island's top producers of charcuterie. ✆ Rue Bonaparte • Map P2

3 Bocca Fina, Propriano
Deli selling superb terrines. ✆ 11 Rue des Pêcheurs • Map J5 • 04957 62810

4 Bergerie d'Acciola, near Sartène
Restaurant and dairy serving Sartenais cheese crêpes and bakes (see p83).

5 L'Orriu, Porto-Vecchio
Top-notch local charcuterie and mountain cheese. ✆ 5 Cours Napoleon • Map L5 • Open Apr–Oct 9am–12:30pm, 3–8:30pm

6 Farmers' Market, Bastia
The gastronomic heart of the city. ✆ Place de l'Hôtel de Ville • MapP5 • Open 7am–1pm Sat–Sun

7 U Paese, Bastia
Fine charcuterie, cheese and wine from Castagniccia. ✆ 4 Rue Napoleon • Map P5 • Open Mar–Oct 9:30am–8pm

8 Marché Couvert, L'Île Rousse
A good variety of Corsican produce. ✆ Place Paoli • Map C4 • Open 8am–1pm

9 A Loghja, Calvi
Shop selling high-class produce from local suppliers. ✆ 3 Rue Clemenceau • Map B4 • 04956 53993 • Open 9:30am–8pm Mar–Oct

10 Alimentation Ghionga, Corte
A fresh-produce shop with old-fashioned displays. ✆ 9 Rue de Vieux Marché • Map D6 • Open 9:30am–7pm Mon–Sat

Corsica's Top 10

Left **Grape harvesting, Domaine de Torraccia** Centre **Cellar, Domaine Saparale** Right **Grapes**

🔟 Wineries

Domaine de Torraccia
Christian Imbert was among the first to recognize the potential of Corsica's traditional vine stock and granitic soil in the 1960s. Grown organically, his hand-harvested grapes produce wines of great distinction. Pick up a bottle of their benchmark "Oriu", regarded as Corsica's finest red. ✎ *Lecci, near Porto-Vecchio • Map L5 • 04957 14350 • www.domaine-de-torraccia.com*

Domaine Saparale
You can taste the crisp minerals of the Vallée de l'Ortolo in Philipe Farinelli's light-bodied wines. Buried deep in one of the wildest corners of the Sartenais, the Domaine underwent massive renovation to bring it into the modern era. Their rosé garners rave reviews *(see pp14–15)*.

Domaine Fiumicicoli
A medieval pack-horse bridge is the symbol of the Propriano area's star winery. Aged in American oak

Domaine Antoine Arena, vineyard

barrels, the red cuvée, Vassilia, is the flagship wine, but of equal pride are the herb-tinged white and red muscat desert wines. ✎ *Marina, near Propriano • Map J5 • 04957 61408*

Domaine Comte Abbatucci
Count Jean-Charles Abbatucci cultivates authentic, unique Corsican grape varieties at this ancestral vineyard, among Corsica's oldest. His vanguard is the white "Faustina" cuvée, a fresh wine with hints of citrus and wild herbs made from 40-year-old vines. ✎ *Pont de Calzola, Chiesale, Casalabriva, Valinco • Map J4 • 04957 40455• Boutique open Jul–Aug 9am–noon, 4–8pm, or by appt • www.domaine-abbatucci.com*

Domaine Antoine Arena
Dodgy local politics have kept this excellent domaine off the AOC list, but its wine is truly sublime – an expression of Corsican viticulture, identity and family values. Handed down father-to-son for generations, the growing techniques have not changed over the years and neither have the wines. Try the inky Niellucciu red. ✎ *Morta Maio, Patrimonio • Map E3 • 04953 70827 • Visits by appt only • www.antoine-arena.fr*

Domaine Gentile
Classic Corsican wines, including one of the island's top

AOC (Appellation d'Origine Contrôlée) is the certification given to French geographical indications for wine and agricultural products.

muscats, are produced by hand according to strict organic principles in this region. The well-drained chalk-schist soil and optimum climate are perfect for wine-making and the wines them-selves are magnificent. ✎ *Olzo, near St-Florent • Map E3 • 04953 70154 • www.domaine-gentile.com*

7 Domaine Leccia
The Corsican grape varieties, Niellucciu (for reds) and Verminto (for whites), combine beautifully with the *terroir* of this third-generation vineyard in the hills outside St-Florent, now in the capable hands of Annette Leccia. State-of-the-art production methods complement a traditional growing style to produce award-winning vintages. ✎ *Poggio d'Oletta, Morta-Piana, near St-Florent • Map E3 • 04953 71135 • Open 9am–7pm Mon–Sat, 10am–6pm Sun • www.domaine-leccia.com*

8 Clos Nicrosi
This 25-acre vineyard in northern Cap Corse retains a distinctly Genoese overtone. The characterful wines it produces are much sought-after but notoriously difficult to find unless you travel to Macinaggio yourself. Their white has a serious following among local wine buffs. ✎ *Rogliano, Macinaggio, Cap Corse • Map E1 • 04953 54117 • Open 10am–noon, 4–7pm Mon–Sat • www.closnicrosi.fr*

9 Domaine Pieretti
Lina Pieretti became the family's fifth-generation winemaker in the late 1980s. The wines now produced owe their distinctiveness to the unusual mix of Alicante and Niellucciu grapes, which thrive in the cape's dry, windy climate. Look out for the orange-scented muscat and earthy red. ✎ *Santa Severa, Luri, Cap Corse • Map E2 • 04953 50103 • Visits by appt only • www.vinpieretti.com*

Wine samples, Clos Culombu

10 Clos Culombu
On the outskirts of Lumio *(see p25),* Etienne Suzzoni's organic vineyards tend towards quality over quantity. The aromatic wines have a strong Corsican character. Enjoy the pink-grey rosé with local snapper; the red comes oaked as "Clos Cuvée" or the more traditional "Domaine". ✎ *Chemin San Pedru, Lumio, near Calvi • Map B4 • 04956 07068 • Open Apr–Oct: 9:30am–1pm, 2–6:30pm Mon–Sat; 10:30am–12:30pm, 3:30–5:30pm Sun • www.closculombu.fr*

Left **Dining hall, Les Roches Rouges** Right **Casa Musicale**

TOP 10 Restaurants

1 Ferme-Auberge Campo di Monte, Murato
Getting to this farmhouse, in the Nebbio hills above St-Florent, is an adventure in itself, and Madame Juillard's traditional cooking – veal in olives, river trout stuffed with *brocciu* and beignets – doesn't disappoint. Ask for a table on the terrace with views of the gulf *(see p99)*.

2 Casa Musicale, Pigna
The delightful Casa Musicale acts as a custodian of the region's culture, and everything you eat here – from the fish, to the grilled meats, honey, fruit and vegetables – originates in the immediate vicinity. Live Corsican music takes over after the liqueurs *(see p99)*.

3 L'Oggi, Lumio
On a stylish terrace looking across the gulf of Calvi, L'Oggi is a Michelin-starred hotel-restaurant serving modern cuisine with a strong French-Corsican accent. It offers four differently priced fixed menus, including one featuring exotic flavours from around the world *(see p99)*.

4 Le Pirate, Erbalunga
Try lobster tortellini with shellfish cream and sprinklings of roasted hazelnuts, or the fragrant octopus

risotto, simmered in squid ink at this Michelin-starred restaurant. Book well in advance *(see p99)*.

5 Le Pasquale Paoli, L'Île Rousse
The owners of this restaurant are proud of their Michelin star, earned for their innovative take on Corsican cuisine. The octopus in olive oil and lemon *confit* gets consistently rave reviews, but there are delightful vegetarian choices as well *(see p99)*.

6 Palm Beach, Ajaccio
This Michelin-starred restaurant is one place you can be assured of fine cooking. The menu is *haute gastronomie* and the quail stuffed with foie gras, on a bed of fetuccini with juice made from wild myrtle leaves, is unmissable *(see p75)*.

7 Les Roches Rouges, Piana
Fine seafood from the Golfe de Porto is the forté of this elegant restaurant on the

Terrace overlooking the Erbalunga harbour, Le Pirate

outskirts of Piana. Try the Scandola lobster (the regional delicacy) or the relatively less expensive local crayfish, served by black-tie waiters in a sunny 1900s dining hall *(see p75)*.

A Pignata, Alta Rocca
Fabulous local cuisine is served in this idyllic rural setting. If it is on the menu, go for the perfect slow-roasted lamb with *cannelloni au brocciu*. There are guest rooms if you are tempted by the wine list *(see p83)*.

A Pignata

L'Altru Versu, Ajaccio
This is Corsican fine dining that relies on the strength of its ingredients. Signature dishes include fish from the gulf baked with *brocciu* and clementine oil, veal with wild mushrooms and lemon and *brocciu* tart with mountain thyme and saffron sorbet. Reservations are essential *(see p75)*.

Le Bélvèdere, Côti-Chiavari
Typical Corsican home-style cooking, with dishes such as grilled wild boar and chestnut-flour polenta, is served on a terrace with a phenomenal view encompassing the entire gulf of Ajaccio and its mountainous hinterland. Moreover, eating here could turn out to be relatively economical, though you will need to reserve well in advance *(see p75)*.

Top 10 Spots for an Apéritif

1 Bar du Quai, Bonifacio
Unassuming café-bar on the sunny side of Bonifacio's busy waterfront. ✆ *Quai Comparetti, Bonifacio • Map K7*

2 Place St-Nicholas, Bastia
The social hub of Bastia, this square is lined with terrace cafés where the town's beau monde congregates. ✆ *Map F3*

3 Place des Portes, St-Florent
Watch the world go by over a chilled glass of local muscat wine in this square. ✆ *Map E3*

4 Place Porta, Sartène
Ancient stone square where the town's social life is played out. ✆ *Map J5*

5 Place Gaffori, Corte
A great space to linger over a coffee in the heart of Corte's crumbling Genoese old town. ✆ *Map D6*

6 Quai Landry, Calvi
Calvi at its swankiest – Côte d'Azur panache with a quintessentially Corsican backdrop. ✆ *Map B4*

7 Le Refuge, Cartalavono
Experience the unique atmosphere of south Corsica's high pine forest at this lodge. ✆ *Massif de l'Ospédale • Map K5 • 04957 00039 • Closed Nov–Mar*

8 Auberge du Col de Bavella
Restaurant with a sunny roadside terrace, with views of the Bavella needles through the trees *(see p83)*.

9 Le Chalet, Haut-Asco
Admire the mighty Monte Cinto over an ice-cold Pietra beer at this ski resort. ✆ *Haut-Asco • Map C5 • 04954 78108 • Open noon–2:30pm, 7:30–10pm • www.hotel-lechalet-asco.com*

10 Place de la République, Porto-Vecchio
Pretty Genoese square where visiting Italians show off their tans and designer clothes in summer. ✆ *Map L5*

AROUND CORSICA

CORSICA'S TOP 10

Left **Calanche rock formations, Piana** Right **Genoese watchtower, Capo di Muro**

Ajaccio and the West Coast

AJACCIO, CORSICA'S FLAMBOYANT CAPITAL, *has two distinct facets: the touristy imperial city, with its pastel-washed alleyways and pretty fishing harbour, and the suburbs of tower blocks spilling up the surrounding hills. The two inhabit largely separate worlds. Few visitors stray further from the waterfront than the 18th-century streets of the old quarter, where Napoleon grew up. The Bonapartes' house and the Palais Fesch, with its landmark collection of Renaissance art, are the city's two principal sights. Both are easily reached in a daytrip from the resorts on the southern shore of the gulf. Further north, the landscape grows increasingly spectacular as you approach the Golfe de Porto, whose orange cliffs are the undisputed scenic highlight of the west coast.*

Statue of Napoleon, Ajaccio

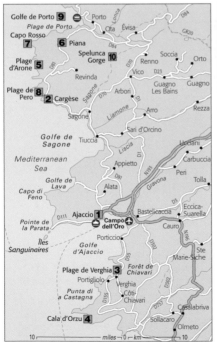

🔟 Sights

1. Ajaccio
2. Cargèse
3. Plage de Verghia
4. Cala d'Orzu
5. Plage d'Arone
6. Piana
7. Capo Rosso
8. Plage de Pero
9. Golfe de Porto
10. Spelunca Gorge

Ajaccio

1 A winter livestock market in Roman times, Ajaccio became a major settlement only after the Genoese erected a Citadelle here in the late 15th century. It expanded rapidly from 1580, and by the mid-17th century had become Corsica's foremost port. Today, it serves

Boats moored in Ajaccio's harbour

as Corsica's main tourist gateway. Above all else, it is famous as being the birthplace of Napoleon, a connection underlined by statues of the "Little Corporal" dominating the town's squares (see pp8–11).

Cargèse

2 In the 17th century, some 730 refugees from a bloody vendetta in the southern Peloponnese alighted on Corsica's west coast near Cargèse. Four hundred years on, their descendents are still here, living in a cluster of neat stone houses ranged around the village's two

The neat rooftops of Cargèse

churches – one Latin Catholic, one Greek Orthodox. The Greek church, Ste-Spyridon, holds original icons brought from Mani in 1676, including a 12th-century Virgin and Child. ◈ Map G1 • www.cargese.net

Plage de Verghia

3 Lying at the very end of the bus route from Ajaccio, this is the least frequented of the sandy bays along the Rive Sud, and by far the prettiest. Shallow, crystal-clear water and powdery white sand makes it a perfect choice for young families and there's plenty of shade in the pine trees crowning the headland to the west. One of the island's more welcoming beach cafés, Mare e Sol serves cold beers on the dune behind. ◈ Map H4

Cala d'Orzu

4 After the manicured beaches of the Rive Sud, Cala d'Orzu offers a distinct change of tone. The atmosphere here is ruled by the churning waves of nearby Capo di Muro (see p74), where a lighthouse surveys a shoreline that feels a million miles from the Riviera chic of Ajaccio. The bay and its adjacent coves are great snorkelling spots and are deserted most weekdays. ◈ Map H4

Genoese Bridges

A typical feature of Corsica's rural landscape are the Genoese bridges over many of its rivers. Although some of these steeply sloping, single-span structures were built in the 13th century, most of them date from the 15th and 16th centuries, when the booming trade in chestnut flower, timber and wine required year-round crossing points.

Ste-Pierre-et-Paul, Piana

Plage d'Arone

5 This heavenly beach lies at the foot of a sweep of deserted mountains below Piana, reached via the D824. Swimming in turquoise water amid such imposing scenery is an experience hard to beat. There is very little else nearby except for a camp site and a few pleasant café-restaurants overlooking the beach. The path winding through the maquis from the north side of the bay leads to a rocky headland from where the views north to Capo Rosso are magnificent. ✎ *Map A7*

Piana

6 Piana *(see p29)* has served as the principal springboard for tours to the nearby Calanche rocks since long before the Corniche was surfaced. Its flower-filled 17th-century square still attracts a steady stream of

visitors in summer. There is nothing much to do here beyond penning a postcard or two on a sunny café terrace, though explorations of the village's cacti-infested fringes reveal spellbinding vistas of the gulf. If you are here at Easter, do not miss the Granitola procession of hooded penitents, starting at the picturesque Ste-Pierre-et-Paul church.

Capo Rosso

7 The southerly of the Herculean red promontories standing guard at the mouth of the Golfe de Porto, Capo Rosso forms a classic humpback shape, its salmon-red cliffs rising vertically from the waves to a solitary Genoese watchtower. The panoramic views from the top are unbelievably beautiful, but it is a long, steep climb. Taking around three hours to walk to the top and back, the path starts 7 km (4 miles) west of Piana on the D824. ✎ *Map A7*

The salmon-red cliffs of Capo Rosso, Golfe de Sagone

Plage de Pero

8 Backed by a scattering of hotels and holiday villas, this well-sheltered bay north of Cargèse makes a great pit stop on long journeys up the west coast. After a dip in its transparent water, stretch your legs with a walk to a 17th-century Genoese watchtower perched on the tip of the headland to the north. Fine views from the tower extend up the coast. ✎ *Map G1*

View of the headland, Plage de Pero

Golfe de Porto

9 The west coast's prime visitor attraction, the Golfe de Porto is unique in the Mediterranean for its red porphyry landscapes. The views extending across the sapphire waters of the bay to the molten red headlands of Scandola and Capo Rosso are unforgettable. Edward Lear, who travelled through the area in 1868, was amazed by its grandeur, rendering the scenery in a series of remarkable line drawings *(see pp28–9)*.

Spelunca Gorge

10 The cliffs of the Spelunca Gorge reach a height of 1000 m (3,280 ft), soaring above a wild valley carpeted in forest and maquis. You can enjoy the landscape by following the old paved trails winding through the gorge, or from the depths of a pool in the river on the valley floor. ✎ *Map B7*

Walking Tour: Ajaccio

Morning

🕐 Kick-start your day's sightseeing at one of the workers' cafés fronting the Place du Marché. From there, follow the narrow backstreet behind the square on to the Rue Fesch, site of the famous **Palais Fesch** *(see pp10–11)*. You will need a good couple of hours to work your way through its highlights. Retracing your steps back down the Rue Fesch, emerge at the palm-lined Place Foch. Napoleon aficionados will love the memorabilia displayed in the **Salon Napoléonien** *(see p9)*, which is a short walk from the Emperor's birthplace, the **Maison Bonaparte** *(see p9)* where you can see the exact divan on which he was born.

🖥 Nearby, the **U Stazzu** deli *(see p61)* is one of the city's most reputed Corsican-produce shops, selling fine charcuterie, wines and honey.

Afternoon

🍴 Pause for lunch at one of the quayside restaurants on the Port Tino Rossi, then follow the road skirting the Genoese **Citadelle** *(see p8)* and St François beach until you see the **Ajaccio Cathedral** *(see p9)* on your right, worth a visit for its moody Delacroix painting inside the doorway. A short walk from there across the Place De Gaulle, dominated by a statue of Napoleon and his brothers, brings you to Ajaccio's main shopping street, Cours Napoléon, where **Grand Café Napoléon** *(see p75)* provides a haven from the mêlée of the town centre.

Left **Plage de Gradelle** Centre **Tortoises, A Cupulatta sanctuary** Right **Col de Verghio**

⁙⁙ Best of the Rest

1 A Cupulatta
This sanctuary is home to a world-renowned collection of tortoises and other reptiles, from Jurassic-looking giants to teeny terrapins. It lies half an hour's drive northeast of Ajaccio on the N193.
◈ *Vignola, Vero, Ucciani, 17 km northeast of Ajaccio • Map J2 • 04955 28234 • Open Apr–mid-May & mid-Sep–Oct: 10am–5pm; mid-May–mid-Sep 9am–7pm • Adm*

2 Porticcio
The largest of the Rive Sud's ribbon of resorts, Porticcio is centered on a broad, sandy beach. Take a bus from Ajaccio or hop on a boat from the old port to get here. ◈ *Map H3*

3 Portigliolo
This idyllic, semi-circular bay at the southwestern extremity of the Golfe d'Ajaccio has a laid-back beach and a well-sheltered snorkelling spot. ◈ *Map H4*

4 Golfe de Sagone
Dip your toes in the water of this spectacular beach at Sagone, the next gulf up the coast from Ajaccio. ◈ *Map G2*

5 Plage de Chiuni
An amazingly secluded bay, Chiuni has a small Club Med complex behind it, but little else to mar its pristine setting. ◈ *Map G1*

6 Pont de Zaglia
This Genoese bridge, located inland from Porto, is where walkers following the trail from Évisa to Ota *(see p47)* come for a spot of swimming. ◈ *Map B7*

7 Le Bélvèdere, Forêt d'Aïtone
This natural balcony formed by boulders at the head of the Spelunca Valley is a great starting point for short walks through the Forêt d'Aïtone. ◈ *Map C7*

8 Plage de Bussaglia
If you are in the Porto area and keen to avoid the crowds, this elegant curve of grey pebbles and blue water, cradled by steep promontories, offers the best retreat. ◈ *Map A6*

9 Plage de Gradelle
Sublime sunset views across the gulf to Capo d'Orto and the Calanche are the chief asset of this relatively unknown beach *(see p29)* at the far northwest end of the Golfe de Porto.

10 Col de Verghio
Head up to the rock-stewn "Pass of the Virgin", dividing the Spelunca and Niolo valleys at the nexus of two major footpaths, for a taste of the watershed's dramatic forests and mountains. ◈ *Map C6*

Left **Chestnut forest around Évisa** Right **Village with the cliffs of Capo d'Orto behind**

🔟 Interior Villages

Ota
Clinging to a steep, maquis-covered hillside above Porto, this classic mountain village of 17th-century granite houses boasts stupendous views across the valley to the north cliffs of Capo d'Orto *(see p29)*. ✎ *Map B7*

Évisa
Chestnut trees and the age-old rhythms of pig rearing govern life in this picturesque hill village above the Spelunca Valley – popular as much for its cuisine as its forest walks. ✎ *Map B7*

Marignana
Marignana's pretty cluster of red-tiled houses with old stone balconies jutting over the chestnut canopy comes as a heavenly vision for walkers on this region's trails. ✎ *Map B7*

Soccia
The tarmac comes to an abrupt end at Soccia, a particularly breathtaking mountain village from where ancient mule tracks, now waymarked for walkers, branch off into the surrounding ridges and forests. ✎ *Map C7*

Renno
A bastion of traditional Corsican hill culture, Renno is one of the island's remotest settlements. Each February, the annual mass pig slaughter provides an excuse for a popular rural fair – "A Tumbera". ✎ *Map C7*

Revinda
Corsica's smallest permanently inhabited village huddles on a lonely hillside above Cargèse *(see p69)*. Aside from the lovely views, the main incentive to visit is to walk to the nearby refuge, E Case *(see p117)*. ✎ *Map B7*

Vico
To escape the tourist trail completely, head 15 km (9 miles) inland from Sagone to Vico, whose medieval, café-lined square holds plenty of gritty Corsican atmosphere. ✎ *Map H1*

Côti-Chiavari
An unforgettable panorama of sea and mountains unfolds from Côti-Chiavari. Its pale-grey houses, reached via a tortuous series of switchbacks from the Rive Sud, straddle high above the Golfe d'Ajaccio. ✎ *Map H4*

Tolla
For a total change of vibe from Ajaccio, head east up the Gorges du Prunelli to Tolla, a sleepy granite village overlooking a huge spread of lake and craggy mountains. ✎ *Map J2*

Guagno-les-Bains
Pascal Paoli numbered among the patrons of this historic spa in the Sagone hinterland, whose thermal, sulphurous waters remain a sought-after cure for rheumatic and skin disorders. ✎ *Map J1*

Left **Col de la Croix to Girolata trail** Centre **The village of Évisa** Right **Capo di Muro**

Day Walks

1 Évisa to Pont de Zaglia
Follow a zigzagging medieval track, with its original cobbles intact, through chestnut and oak forest to this Genoese packhorse bridge *(see p72)*, where you can bathe in the river. ➲ *Map B7*

2 Ota to Serreira
One of the benchmark stages of the Tra Mare e Monti Nord trail *(see p46)*, this route winds the 900-m (2,950-ft) high San Petru pass. Enjoy the marvellous panorama over the Golfe de Porto. ➲ *Map A7*

3 Évisa to Marignana
This leisurely amble through the leafy woodland separating two of the island's loveliest villages makes for an ideal out-and-back day walk. Stop for lunch at the cheerful Ustaria di a Rota *(see p117)*. ➲ *Map B7*

4 Col de Verghio to Cascades de Radule
An immensely enjoyable hike over the sun-drenched, rocky terrain of the upper Golo Valley brings you to a blue-green pool fed by a perennial waterfall. This is a lovely spot to swim in the water and sunbathe. ➲ *Map C6*

5 Col de la Croix to Girolata
This classic Corsican three-hour hike takes you from the Golfe de Porto's Corniche to the coastal village of Girolata, via hillsides of dense maquis and a flotsam-covered cove. ➲ *Map A6*

6 Château Fort
A colossal chunk of red porphyry resembling a castle, the Château Fort marks the end point of a varied, hour-long jaunt north of the Roches Bleues café, through the Calanches rock formations. ➲ *Map B7*

7 Sentier Muletier
A small oratory in the cliff, 500 m (1,640 ft) south of the Roches Bleues café, flags the head of this more strenuous trail through the Calanches via the old path formerly connecting Ota and Piana. ➲ *Map B7*

8 Capo d'Orto
An immense 360-degree panorama over Corsica's most awesome landscape is the reward for ascending Capo d'Orto, the sugar-loaf summit looming above Porto. The trail starts 1.5 km (1 mile) east of Piana. ➲ *Map B7*

9 Chemin des Crêtes
A superb ridge route, the Chemin des Crêtes slices uphill from Ajaccio to follow the rocky spine of the mountain that rises behind the city. ➲ *Map H3*

10 Capo di Muro
This is the nearest stretch of wild coast you come to if you track the shoreline south from Ajaccio. An old watchtower makes the perfect target for a walk along the headland *(see p41)*. ➲ *Map H4*

Price Categories

For a three-course meal for one with half a bottle of wine (or equivalent meal), taxes and extra charges.

€	under €20
€€	€20–€30
€€€	€30–€40
€€€€	€40–€50
€€€€€	over €50

Left **Grand Café Napoléon**

🔟 Restaurants

1 Grand Café Napoléon
Have a pastry in the tearoom, or fine dine in the sumptuous Second Empire restaurant in Ajaccio's most elegant meeting place. ⊗ *10 Cours Napoléon, Ajaccio • Map P2 • 04952 14254 • €€€€€*

2 Palm Beach
Riding high on its Michelin star, this designer restaurant on the swanky Rive Nord offers a refined and sophisticated menu. ⊗ *Route des Sanguinaires, Ajaccio • Map H3 • 049 55 20103 • Closed Sun pm & Mon • €€€€€*

3 L'Altru Versu
This restaurant, offering a refined, gourmet take on traditional Corsican mountain cuisine, is the first choice for serious foodies in the capital. ⊗ *Les Sept Chapelles, Route des Sanguinaires, Ajaccio • Map H3 • 04955 00522 • Open noon–8pm daily (Thu–Mon mid-Oct–mid-Jun); Closed Feb • €€€€€*

4 Le Spago
A trendy lounge bar-restaurant just off the Cours Napoléon, Le Spago serves an eclectic menu. It hosts DJs and live bands at weekends.⊗ *1 Rue Emmanuel Arène, Ajaccio • Map P2 • 04952 11571 • €€*

5 Le Bélvèdere
This restaurant, in a bed-and-breakfast high above the Rive Sud, has fantastic views from its terrace. The home cooking is delicious. ⊗ *Côti-Chiavari • Map H4 • 04952 71032 • Open Mar–mid-Nov: 7:30–9pm daily; Mar–May: Sun lunch • €€€*

6 Les Roches Rouges
Gourmet cuisine is served here in a frescoed, *fin-de-siècle* dining hall with sublime views. ⊗ *Piana, Golfe de Porto • Map A7 • 04952 78181 • Open Mar–Nov • €€€€€ • www.lesrochesrouges.com*

7 A Casa Corsa, Piana
Choose your own lobster at this fresh seafood restaurant offering sunset views of the Piana Calanche. ⊗ *Route de Porto, Piana • Map A7 • 04952 45793 • Open 7am–midnight • €€€€*

8 L'Arbousier
High Gallic gastronomy, made from local ingredients by chef Gérard Lorenzini, is served here on a terrace overlooking a private beach. ⊗ *Le Maquis, Porticcio • Map H3 • 04952 52015 • Open noon–2pm, 8–10pm • €€€€€ • www.lemaquis.com*

9 A Tramula
Relish the charcuterie, veal and chestnut dishes along with other mountain delights on offer at A Tramula. Ask for a table on the balcony overlooking the valley. ⊗ *Évisa • Map B7 • 04952 62439 • €€€€*

10 A Merendella
Fragrant charcuterie, *figatellu* (Corsican sausage) with melted *brocciu* and sautéd veal with chestnut honey are among the specialities of this restaurant, hidden up a side valley inland from Sagone. ⊗ *Piazza al Brignone, Soccia • Map C7 • 04952 83491 • Open May–Sep: noon–1:30pm, 8–9:30pm • €€€*

Left **Limestone cliff, near Bonifacio** Centre **Sartène museum** Right **Statue-menhir, Filitosa**

Bonifacio and the South

THE SPECTACLE OF BONIFACIO'S *striated chalk cliffs rising from the sea to its crown of medieval walls is an arresting sight. Set against a backdrop of deserted maquis, the town possesses an exotic atmosphere. Nearly everyone holidaying around this area's magnificent shell-sand beaches visits Bonifacio, though it is frequently upstaged as the region's hub by nearby Porto-Vecchio, another former Genoese stronghold. Inland, a giant wall of boulder-studded hills and maritime pine forest separates the coast from the villages of the Alta Rocca, whose steep, wooded valleys sprawl west into the Golfe de Valinco below the medieval skyline of Sartène.*

The Citadelle, Bonifacio

🔟 Sights

1 Bonifacio
2 Golfe de Valinco
3 Îles Lavezzi
4 Sartène
5 Alta Rocca
6 Route de Bavella
7 Pianu di Levie (Cucuruzzu)
8 Aiguilles de Bavella
9 Porto-Vecchio
🔟 Plage de Palombaggia

Preceding pages **Ferry ride from Ajaccio to Capo d'Orto**

Bonifacio

1 Seemingly about to collapse into the blue waters of the Straits, this old Genoese town withstood repeated sieges by the Aragonese and, in 1554, a Turkish fleet led by the corsair Dragut *(see p29)*. Today, Bonifacio's dramatic harbour, clifftop Citadelle and chalk escarpments attract visitors all year round. From July through September its cobbled alleyways become totally swamped – all the more reason to hop on one of the excursion boats chugging out of the port below to view the *haute ville* from sea level *(see pp16–17)*.

Golfe de Valinco

2 The serene beaches on both the northern and southern shores of the Golfe de Valinco are the main reason people base themselves in the southwest of the island, but there are many interesting sights inland to tempt you away from the coast – not least the famous prehistoric site of Filitosa. Catch an excursion boat from Propriano to explore this area's wild coves, surveyed by Genoese watchtowers, a legacy of the pirate raids which forced the local population into the hills in the 15th and 16th centuries *(see pp12–13)*.

Granite rocks, Îles Lavezzi

Îles Lavezzi

3 This cluster of low granite-rock islets off Bonifacio rests amid superbly transparent water. Boats shuttle here throughout the day in season, allowing plenty of time for snorkelling and for exploring the archipelago's winding pathways and hidden coves. The only structures of note are the walled Cimetière Archiano, where victims of the 1855 shipwreck of the Sémillante *(see p17)* are buried, and a memorial to the disaster. Bring refreshments along, as there are no cafés on the islands. ◈ *Map L7*

Sartène

4 The playwright Prosper Mérimée famously dubbed Sartène as "the most Corsican of Corsican towns" – though whether he was referring to its austere appearance or the grim-faced demeanour of its inhabitants is a moot point. Enjoy an apéritif on the ancient Place Porta, where the locals congregate for a postprandial walk, followed by a wander around the narrow back alleys. The town's museum boasts the island's largest collection of prehistoric artifacts *(see pp14–15)*.

Porto-Pollo beach, Golfe de Valinco

Grouper Fish

The famously clear waters in the Straits of Bonifacio off the Îles Lavezzi are home to a colony of extraordinary fish. Tamed by decades of visits, the large shoal of grouper used to take morsels from the hands of divers, a practice that has been banned. The colony is now protected as part of the Réserve Naturelle des Bouches de Bonifacio.

View from the Route de Bavella

5 Alta Rocca

The hilly interior of southern Corsica is known as the Alta Rocca. With its deep river valleys, lush forests of chestnut and oak and ancient granite villages, it is a world away from the coast. The old paved mule trails and the Mare a Mare Sud hiking route *(see p46)* are a great way to explore the area, but you can cover the highlights in a day-long driving tour, stopping for swims, woodland strolls and platters of mountain charcuterie on village squares along the way. ◈ *Map K4*

Ste-Lucie de Tallano village in the Alta Rocca

6 Route de Bavella

One of Corsica's most scenic roads, the Route de Bavella winds inland from Solenzara on the southeast coast, approaching the famous Aiguilles via a series of cliffs, forests and gorges. Be warned though, that despite attempts to widen the road, slow-moving vehicles impede progress in high season, so try to get an early start. ◈ *Map L3*

7 Pianu di Levie (Cucuruzzu)

Savour the atmosphere and distinctive landscape of the Alta Rocca region from the ramparts of this Bronze Age castle, with its vaulted chambers, stairways, hearths and granaries still intact. The site, inhabited around 1400 BC, is set amid ancient holm oak forest, with views of the distant Aiguilles de Bavella to the north-east. A 20-minute walk north through the woods leads to the monument A Capula, occupied until 1259, where a Romanesque chapel stands in a clearing. ◈ *Map K4 • 04957 84821 • Open Apr–Oct: 9:30am–6pm (to 7pm Jun–Sep; to 8pm Jul–Aug); Nov–Mar: for group bookings only • Adm*

8 Aiguilles de Bavella

Rising from the Corsican watershed on the opposite side of the valley from Monte Incudine, the Aiguilles de Bavella are giant towers of tapering granite, the stacks visible for miles in every direction, lending a serrated appearance to the skyline inland from Porto-Vecchio. Yellow waymarks flag a scrambling route up to and around the bases – a variant of the GR20 trekking trail, for which the needles provide a stunning closing stretch. ◈ *Map K4*

Porto-Vecchio

9 The Genoese developed Porto-Vecchio in 1539 as a harbour from which to ship Corsican cork to the Italian mainland. Afflicted by malaria-carrying mosquitoes, it was seen abandoned, but has been a resurgence since World War II owing to its proximity to some of the island's finest beaches. Chic boutiques pitched at high-rolling Italians line the *haute ville's* medieval streets, which converge on a cheerful church square filled with the aroma of fresh croissants and coffee in the mornings. ✪ *Map L5*

Boats moored in Porto-Vecchio harbour

Plage de Palombaggia

10 The turquoise water and soft white sand at Palombaggia make for a picture-perfect setting. The beach here actually comprises three contiguous bays, separated by headlands crowned by clumps of umbrella and maritime pines. Palombaggia is the most northerly of the trio and the best for watersports; next comes Tamaricciu, with its stylish café-restaurant made out of teak; and finally, Accario, the smallest and quietest. ✪ *Map L6*

Route de Bavella and Massif de l'Ospédale

Morning

🕐 This circular driving tour takes in the scenic highlights of the mountain area inland from Porto-Vecchio. Leave town on the main Bastia road (RN198) and follow it as far as **Solenzara** *(see p88)*, where the D268 turns left off the highway, winding southwest above the Solenzara river. A striking panorama of forested mountains and cliffs is revealed at the Col de Larone. From there onwards the landscape grows more spectacular at each bend, culminating at the Col de Bavella itself where, in the shadow of the famous **Aiguilles de Bavella**, you can follow a delightful waymarked trail through pine forest to the **Trou de la Bombe** *(see p47)* before enjoying a typical Corsican mountain lunch at the **Auberge du Col de Bavella** *(see p83)*.

Afternoon

A white Notre-Dame-des-Neiges (Our Lady of the Snow) statue presides over the high point of the pass, from where the D268 winds downhill all the way to **Zonza** *(see p39)*, one of the prettiest villages in the high Alta Rocca. From Zonza, follow the D368 into the wooded Massif de l'Ospédale. Beyond the Bocca d'Illarata pass, a café on the left side of the road marks the start of a superb 90-minute walk to the 70-m (230-ft) Piscia di Gallu waterfall. At Ospédale, the next village along the D368, the Vieux Lavoir café has superb views extending all the way to Sardinia.

Left **Holidaymakers at Plage de Pinarello** Right **Ermitage de la Trinté**

Best of the Rest

1 Castellu d'Araggio
High on a rocky hillside to the northwest of Porto-Vecchio, this prehistoric Citadelle enjoys a spectacular setting, with magnificent views extending across the coast. ✆ Map L5

2 Plage de Pinarello
Shallow, pale-blue water, enfolded by a crescent of white sand, makes Pinarello a most attractive beach for families. Easily accessible by road, it gets busy in peak season. ✆ Map L5

3 Quenza
This is a 1000-year-old quintessential Alta Rocca village, where the broad-leaf forest ebbs into the high uplands of the Coscione plateau. A chapel stands on its outskirts. ✆ Map K4

4 Plateau de Coscione
To the north of the Alta Rocca, this upland served as a summer pasture for the region's shepherds for centuries. It now lies deserted, save for the odd walker and horse rider. ✆ Map K3

5 Carbini
Tiny Carbini, at the foot of the Massif de l'Ospédale, is the site of the Pisan church of San Giovanni where, in 1362, a heretical sect was slaughtered on the orders of the Pope. ✆ Map K5

6 Cala di l'Avena
A broad bay lashed by year-round surf, Cala di l'Avena is a good option if you like your beaches wild and windy (see p15). A no-frills campsite behind it provides the essentials. ✆ Map H6

7 Plage de Tralicetu
You have to negotiate a very rough, 4-km (3-mile) track to reach Tralicetu, one of southern Corsica's most remote and unspoilt beaches. Facilities are nonexistent. ✆ Map H6

8 Piantarella
This kitesurfing and sailboarding hot spot to the east of Bonifacio encompasses the most astonishingly turquoise water on the island. ✆ Map L7

9 Ermitage de la Trinité
Huddled beneath a huge granite outcrop, the Ermitage de la Trinité is among the oldest Christian monuments on Corsica. A superb vista extends from its terrace down the coast. ✆ Map K7

10 Plage de Balistra
This is the only beach in the Porto-Vecchio–Bonifacio area where you can be assured plenty of elbow room even at the height of summer. Brave a stretch of badly rutted piste to get here. ✆ Map L7

Around Corsica – Bonifacio and the South

82

Price Categories

For a three course meal for one with half a bottle of wine (or equivalent meal), taxes and extra charges.

€	under €20
€€	€20–€30
€€€	€30–€40
€€€€	€40–€50
€€€€€	over €50

Left **Auberge Santa Barbara**

🔟 Places to Eat

Cantina Doria
Enjoy good local cooking in this restaurant specializing in Corsican cuisine, squeezed into a narrow alley in the *haute ville*. ⊗ *27 Rue Doria, Bonifacio • Map K7 • 04957 35049 • Open Mar–Oct • €€€*

Cantina Grill
Fresh seafood as well as lasagna and other Bonifacian staples are served in this superb location on the waterfront. The prices are reasonable. ⊗ *3 Quai Banda del Ferro, Bonifacio • Map K7 • 04957 04986 • Open Mar–Oct • €€€*

Casa del Mar
Sample the gastronomical delights crafted from Corsican ingredients by Michelin-starred chef Davide Bisetto at this fine restaurant. ⊗ *Route de Palombaggia, near Porto-Vecchio • Map L5 • 04957 23 434 • Open May–Oct: 8–10:30pm • €€€€€*

A Cantina di L'Orriu
Locals and visitors alike enjoy the warm welcome, local grilled veal or an *assiette charcuterie* (cold meats) at this festive and lively wine bar. ⊗ *5, cours Napoleon, Porto-Vecchio • Map L5 • 04952 59589 • Open midday–2pm, 7–11pm • €€€€*

Le Tamaricciu
This beach bistro is known for its fresh salads, pasta dishes and wood-grilled fish. It also serves oven-baked pizzas at lunchtime. ⊗ *Plage Palombaggia, Porto-Vecchio • Map L6 • 04957 04989 • Open mid-Apr–mid-Oct • €€€€€*

Bergerie d'Acciola
Great regional dishes with an accent on local ewes' and goats' cheese can be enjoyed at this terrace restaurant. ⊗ *Orasi, Route de Bonifacio, 8 km south of Sartène • Map J5 • 04957 71400 • Open Jun–Sep • €€*

Auberge du Col de Bavella
GR20 walkers refuel here on peasant soup, mountain charcuterie, grilled lamb, wild boar stew and freshly made desserts. ⊗ *Col de Bavella, Zonza • Map L4 • 04957 20987 • Open Apr–mid-Nov • €€€*

Jardin de l'Échaugette
This is the most relaxing place to eat in central Sartène, where you can enjoy local specialities such as veal stew with chestnut polenta. ⊗ *Place Vardiola • Map J5 • 04957 71286 • Open mid-April–Sep • €€€*

Auberge Santa Barbara
Feast on classic Sartenais dishes here, such as langoustine salad and roast pigeon with wild myrtle berries. ⊗ *Route de Propriano, Sartène • Map J5 • 04957 70906 • Open Apr–Oct • €€€€€*

A Pignata
The splendid views from this farmhouse, looking across the Alta Rocca, are matched by the fragrant rustic cooking. Booking is essential. ⊗ *Route du Pianu, Levie • Map K4 • 04957 84190 • Open Apr–Oct • €€€€*

Left **Balagne coast** Right **Vallée de Niolo**

Corte, the Interior and the East Coast

I F YOU NEVER VENTURE FROM THE COAST, *you are sure to get a distorted impression of Corsica. Inland, the deep, forested valleys of the island's core create a radical shift in tone. Spilling from the foot of an eagle's nest Citadelle, Corte is the largest town in Corsica's interior. Its old town, a warren of red-tiled tenements and churches, presides over a nexus of several major valleys, making it the perfect springboard for forays into the surrounding mountains. The quickest route to Corte is via Aléria* on the east coast. A broad, flat, low-lying plain striped with vineyards and fruit orchards, this is perhaps the least spectacular side of the island, but one which compensates for its scenic shortcomings with some impressive Roman ruins, glorious mountain villages and a vast expanse of relatively unfrequented beaches.

Pascal Paoli overlooking Boulevard Paoli, Corte

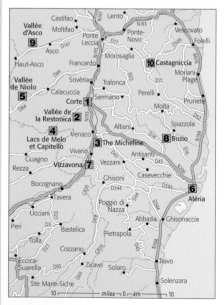

🔟 Sights

Corte

Corte served as the island's capital between 1755 and 1769, when Pascal Paoli made it the seat of his revolutionary government. With its imposing mountain backdrop and Moor's Head flags fluttering above an 18th-century old town, Corte still retains an aura of nationalist defiance. Bullet holes made by Genoese beseigers pockmark the walls of the cobbled square below the Citadelle, where Corsican-speaking students from the nearby university crowd the bars in term time. ✎ Map D6

View of the old town and Citadelle, Corte

picnic spots, while a network of old shepherds' trails provides a great opportunity for a walk around the forest. ✎ Map D6

Vallée de la Restonica

Mesmerized by the high ridges soaring above them, few of the visitors pouring up the Vallée de la Restonica spare more than a passing glance at the valley floor, but the river surging across it hides dozens of superb swimming spots. The pale green meltwater cascades through pools hollowed from immense granite boulders known as "vasques". Shady areas under the Laricio pines make perfect

The Micheline

Known affectionately as the "Micheline", Corsica's little train forms an essential, year-round, all-weather link between Ajaccio and Bastia. The route, built in the 19th century and upgraded in 2008, is breathtakingly scenic – especially the stretch branching northwest to Calvi from Ponte Leccia, which skirts the fabulous Balagne coastline. Catch one of the four daily services to Vizzavona from Corte – a 40-minute ride through pine forests and picturesque villages, with a crossing of the famous Pont de Vecchiu bridge en route. ✎ Map D5

Lacs de Melo et Capitello

The dramatic Vallée de la Restonica scythes from the outskirts of Corte into the heart of the watershed – one of the Mediterranean's great mountain wildernesses. In summer, streams of visitors drive or catch the shuttle bus to the car park at the end of the valley, from where a magnificent trail winds up inclined slabs and scree slopes to a pair of beautiful glacial lakes, surrounded by a vast stadium of cliffs. Visit before the snow melts in early May to see the lakes partly frozen. ✎ Map D7

The Restonica river surging around rocks

Corsican Polyphony

Corsica boasts its own distinctive brand of choral music – known locally as "polyphonies corses". The style, which hinges on three or four parts, evolved a means of singing Mass in remote shepherds' villages, but has since become the backbone of a vibrant and popular musical revival led by groups such as I Muvrini and A Filetta.

Roman ruins, Aléria

Vallée de Niolo

Corsica's most remote mountain region is the Vallée de Niolo. Its heart, spread below the eroded southern fringes of Monte Cinto *(see p57)*, is a broad depression scattered with granite villages where vestiges of the old transhumant culture that formerly held sway here are still discernable. The local ewe's cheese is mouth-wateringly good and walking is superlative, whatever your level of capability. If you are in the area in September, do not miss the annual fair, Santa di u Niolu *(see p43)*. ✎ *Map C6*

Aléria

Located at the mouth of the Tavignano river on the eastern coastal plain, Aléria was a major Greek and Roman colony in ancient times, when the Étang de Diane lagoon below it functioned as the island's main harbour and naval base *(see p88)*. Ruins of the former Roman town, which include baths, a forum and triumphal archway, are spread over a hilltop to the south of the modern village, set against a wonderful backdrop of cloud-swept mountains. Foodies can dine on oysters from the nearby *étang* (pond). ✎ *Map M1*

Vizzavona

A collection of tin-roofed railway buildings and forestry huts, Vizzavona is the highest stop on Corsica's diminutive train line – a perfect springboard for walks in the magnificent Laricio pine forest. Picnickers meander through the woods to the Cascade des Anglais waterfall *(see p51)*, while those with more stamina and a head for heights scale the colossal Monte d'Oro, whose grey-blue cliffs and pointed summit are this area's defining landmark. ✎ *Map K1*

Bozio

This micro region, overlooking the Vallée du Tavignano *(see p27)* to the southeast of Corte, sees very few visitors, but is a great area for getting a feel of traditional mountain life. Clustered along the course of the old via Romana, a string

The lush forest around Vizzavona

of picturesque stone villages looks across the valley to Monte Rotondo. The Mare a Mare Centre hiking trail winds through the area, undulating between deserted uplands and ruined sheepfolds. ✎ *Map E7*

9 Vallée d'Asco

The head of the Asco Valley, known as Haut-Asco, is flanked by Corsica's highest mountains, including Monte Cinto. It was here, amid the vast pines and boulder moraines, that Felix von Cube and the other early pioneers of Corsican mountaineering made their base camp in the 1900s while forging routes up the surrounding peaks. The wood-lined bar in the ski station here displays antique photos of the explorers and you can admire the awesome crags opposite from the comfort of a sun-drenched café terrace. ✎ *Map C5*

Snow-covered peak of Monte Cinto

10 Castagniccia

Swathed in a dense canopy of chestnut forest, Castagniccia, in the northeast of the island, has an entirely different feel to it. The intense greenery ensures a moist climate and in autumn, when the woods are ablaze with colour, mist cloaks the valley floor most mornings. Splendid baroque churches, great walks around the forest and the pungent local charcuterie draw visitors here. ✎ *Map E5*

Circular Route: Corte–Aléria–Corte

Morning

🕐 This round route loops through some of the least visited, but most scenic corners of central and eastern Corsica. Begin by heading south from **Corte** *(see p85)* on the main Ajaccio highway (RN193). After 33 km (21 miles), just beyond Vivario, turn left on to the D69 at the **Col de la Serra Piana** *(see p89)* to start the ascent of the 1311-m (4,300-ft) high Col de Sorba. An 11-km (7-mile) drop down the other side brings you to the dramatically sited village of Ghisoni, whose café makes an atmospheric pit stop. From Ghisoni, follow the D344 as it winds through the awesome Défilé de Strette gorge to Ste-Antoine, where you should turn left and follow the D343 across the vineyards to **Aléria**. Tour the hilltop Roman ruins and adjacent museum before heading east to the nearby Plage du Padulone for a swim and bite to eat at one of the beachside *paillotes* (huts). Then continue northwest from Aléria on the N200, turning right on to the D14 after 13 km (8 miles).

Afternoon

This tortuous road follows the course of the old via Romana through the wonderful **Bozio** region – among the most spectacular drives on the island. Head through Pietraserena, Altiani and Erbajolo villages, before dropping back down to the valley floor via the D14. This brings you out on the N200, only 5 km (3 miles) south of Corte.

Left **Village church, Morosaglia** Right **Church campanile, Cervione**

Best of the Rest

1 Pont de Vecchio
Gustave Eiffel was the brains behind the magnificent Pont de Vecchio railway bridge near Vivario – best viewed from the adjacent 222-m (728-ft) road bridge. ✎ Map K1

2 Haut-Asco
Head for the former ski station of Haut-Asco to access the most rugged terrain in Corsica – a vast amphitheatre of red-granite mountains. ✎ Map C5

3 Donkey Rides
The shepherds' paths intersecting the Vallée de Niolo make perfect routes for extended donkey treks into the Corsican mountains. ✎ Promenâne, Albertacce • Map C6 • 06152 94564 • May–Sep • Adm • www.randonee-ane-corse.com

4 Calasima
At 1,100 m (3,609 ft), Calasima is Corsica's highest village – a tiny cluster of cottages dwarfed by the vast spectre of Paglia Orba (see p53) behind. ✎ Map C6

5 Morosaglia
A museum of memorabilia marks the birthplace of Pascal Paoli. His ashes are interred in a chapel next door. ✎ La Maison de Pascal Paoli, Rue Principale, Morosaglia • Map E5 • 04956 10497 • Open 9am–noon, 2:30–7pm (1–5pm in winter); Closed public hols • Adm

6 Casinca
The villages of this region, whose schist-tiled houses spill over ridges of the northeast coast, are a welcome respite from the congested coast in summer. ✎ Map F5

7 Fiumorbo
This region is a lesser-known cluster of beautiful, depopulated villages sprinkled across the hills inland from Ghisonaccia. Drive up for coffee on picturesque squares with views out to sea. ✎ Map L2

8 Étang de Diane
This lagoon outside Aléria has been a source of oysters for centuries. An island in it is made entirely of shells discarded by the Romans. ✎ Map M1

9 Solenzara
The liveliest resort on the east coast, Solenzara has an endless sandy beach and dramatic mountain hinterland. ✎ Map L3

10 Cervione
The largest of the mountain villages surveying the east coast, Cervione boasts a baroque cathedral on its medieval square and an ethnographic museum. ✎ Musée ADECEC, Place Jean Simonetta • Map F6 • Open 10am–noon, 2:30–6pm Mon–Sat • Adm • www.adecec.net/html/musee.html

Left **Lac de Nino** Right **View of snow-capped peaks from Col de Serra Piana**

🔟 Day Walks

Lac de Nino
Scramble up the steep sides of the Vallée de Niolo to reach the largest and most beautiful of Corsica's many glacial lakes, suspended in the middle of green pasture, against a magnificent mountain backdrop. 🔊 *Map C/*

Cascade des Anglais
Accessed via a gentle 20-minute amble through pine forest, this idyllic waterfall is a perfect spot for a picnic, with plenty of pools to splash about in nearby. 🔊 *Map J1*

Cascades de Radule
The landscape takes on a high-mountain feel as you approach the hidden Radule waterfall, just off the GR20 in the Golo river valley. The start point is the car park at Col de Verghio. 🔊 *Map C6*

Gorges du Tavignano
Follow the zigzagging Genoese mule track up this valley near Corte to reach an awesome gorge, carpeted with Laricio pines. Chanterelle mushrooms grow in profusion here in autumn. 🔊 *Map C7*

Lac d'Oriente
The challenging climb up Monte Rotondo may be only for confirmed mountaineering enthusiasts, but this magical glacial lake halfway up is more easily accessible. 🔊 *Map D7*

Col de la Serra Piana
Swim under the old Pont d'Asco Genoese bridge before embarking on a climb up the side valley opposite Asco village to get to a lonely pass offering wonderful views. 🔊 *Map D5*

Gorges de Manganellu
Follow the orange waymarks from the hamlet of Canaglia, 25 km (16 miles) south of Corte, to reach one of the loveliest forested valleys on the island. The remote Bergerie de Tolla makes the perfect turnaround point *(see p90)*. 🔊 *Map D7*

Pont de Muricciolu
On the outskirts of Albertacce village, a Genoese packhorse bridge spans a particularly photogenic stretch of river. Huge, water-worn slabs flank the river, which you can reach in an easy half hour's walk. 🔊 *Map C6*

Punta Muvrella
"Peak of the Sheep" is a superb eagle's nest summit overlooking the Vallée d'Asco *(see p87)* to the Cinto Massif. It is a relentlessly steep three-hour, 700-m (2,296-ft) climb from the Haut-Asco ski station. 🔊 *Map C5*

Tour des Cinqui Frati
This is a classic walk in the Vallée de Niolo *(see p86)*, looping around a phalanx of rock pinnacles. Leaflets detailing the route are on sale at local tourist offices. 🔊 *Map C6*

Left **GR20 hikers resuming their trek from Refuge d'Ortu di u Piobbu** Right **Bergerie d'Asinau**

Top 10 Mountain Huts and Bergeries

1 Refuge d'Ortu di u Piobbu
Ortu is the first refuge you reach after starting on the GR20 mountain walk from Calenzana *(see p46)*. ◈ Map C5 • *04956 28778 • Open Jun–Sep • €17 per dorm bed*

2 Refuge de Carozzu
For GR20 trekkers, Carozzu hoves into view after a knee-crunching descent down a rocky ravine. Its deck is a great spot for a chilled beer. ◈ Map C5 • *Open Jun–Sep • €17 per dorm bed*

3 Refuge Ciottulu a i Mori
The highest refuge in Corsica, Ciottulu perches on a natural balcony at the foot of Paglia Orba. It looks down the majestic Golo Valley from an altitude of just under 2000 m (6,560 ft). ◈ Map C6 • *Open May–Sep • €17 per dorm bed*

4 Bergeries a Vaccaghia
This ancient stone sheepfold, still used throughout the summer by shepherds, provides the nearest permitted bivouac and camping site to Lac de Nino *(see p89)*. It sells very strong cheese. ◈ Map C7 • *Open May–Sep • €17 per dorm bed*

5 Refuge A Sega
A Sega nestles deep in the pine forest midway up the Vallée du Tavignano, around four hours' walk out of Corte. It is an important waymark on the Mare a Mare Centre walk. ◈ Map D6 • *04954 60790, 06107 17726 • Open Apr–Oct • €17 per dorm bed*

6 Refuge U Renoso
This GR20 refuge at the foot of Monte Renoso offers cheaper accommodation than the nearby lodge, as well as hot showers and freshly cooked meals. ◈ Map K2 • *Open May–Sep • €17 per dorm bed*

7 Refuge d'Usciolu
Warden Frances Pantalacce stocks up this refuge every day from down the mountain. It is among the best-run refuges on the GR20 (although drinking water is in low supply July–August). ◈ Map K3 • *Open May–Sep • €17 per dorm bed*

8 Bergerie d'Asinau
A working sheepfold just off the GR20 below the national park's own hut, this bergerie serves terrific mountain cooking. ◈ Map K3 • *06175 39892 • Open Mid-May–Sep • €40 half board*

9 Bergerie de Basetta
Set on the edge of the Plateau de Coscione, this refuge provides rustic accommodation and meals for walkers, in a forest glade about an hour's walk off the GR20. ◈ *Route de Saint-Pierre, 15 km southeast of Zicavo • Map K3 • 06272 59533 • Open mid-Apr–mid-Oct • €38 half board*

10 Bergerie de Tolla
Hidden deep in a wonderful pine forest, up one of the interior's sleepiest valleys, the Bergerie de Tolla serve delicious, calorific snacks and hot meals to hungry walkers. ◈ *Gorges de Manganellu • Map K1 • Open mid-Jun–mid-Sep • €10–€15*

You can book staffed refuges on the GR20 route via the national park's website (www.parc-corse.org).

Price Categories

For a three-course meal for one with half a bottle of wine (or equivalent meal), taxes and extra charges.

€	under €20
€€	€20–€30
€€€	€30–€40
€€€€	€40–€50
€€€€€	over €50

Left **L'Ortu**

🔟 Places to Eat

1 Monte d'Oro
Try traditional mountain cooking at this famous wayside restaurant, located where the main Ajaccio–Bastia highway crosses the watershed. ⊗ *Vivario, near Vizzavona • Map K1 • 04954 72106 • Open May–early Oct • €€€*

2 Bergerie de Tolla
The owner of this sheepfold deep in the forest serves ewe's cheese omelettes, and nuts roasted in chestnut honey *(see p90)*.

3 Auberge de la Restonica
Quality Corsican mountain cuisine, ranging from wild boar stew to fresh trout stuffed with mint, is served at this romantic hotel. ⊗ *Route de la Restonica, 2 km southwest of Corte • Map D6 • 04954 60958 • Open Apr–Oct • €€€€*

4 Osteria di l'Orta
Corsican specialities, such as veal with olives and melt-in-the-mouth chestnut mousse, entice visitors and locals alike to this restaurant in an 18th-century mansion at the north end of town. ⊗ *Casa Guelfucci, Pont de l'Orta, Corte • Map D6 • 04956 10641 • Open Apr–mid-Nov • €€€€*

5 Bienvenue Chez JoJo
Sample charcuterie, rich game stews and chestnut flour desserts, offered at unbeatable rates, in this simple village eatery next to the Calacuccia lake. ⊗ *Albertacce, Vallée de Niolo • Map C6 • 04954 80687 • €€*

6 Restaurant du Lac
Down-to-earth Nioline dishes flavoured with wild mountain herbs, mushrooms and cheese are the specialities here. ⊗ *Sidossi, near Calacuccia, Vallée de Niolo • Map C6 • 04954 80273 • €€*

7 Aux Coquillages de Diana
Shellfish aficionados can tuck into fresh local Nustale oysters and mussels, washed down with a glass of icy Vermentino wine. ⊗ *Étang de Diana, Aléria • Map M1 • 04955 70455 • Open Jun–Sep: daily; Oct–May: lunch daily, dinner Fri–Sat • Closed Jan • €€€*

8 Restaurant de l'Ampugnani
Savour Castagniccian trout, free-range pork stews, herb-tinged local cheese and crunchy *brocciu* beignets in this dining salon that also offers lovely valley views. ⊗ *La Porta, Castagniccia • Map E5 • 04953 92200 • Open 11:30am–10pm daily • €€*

9 U Fragnu
This bistro, specializing in Corsican cuisine, serves huge portions of veal and olive stew, soup with fresh soft cheese and leek and *brocciu* fritters. ⊗ *U Campu, Route de Vescovato, Venzolasca • Map F5 • 04953 66233 • €€€€*

10 L'Ortu
Corsica's only organic eatery, specializing in vegetarian fare, with the odd free-range pork dish thrown in for die-hard carnivores. ⊗ *Route de Venzolasca, Vescovato • Map F5 • 04953 66469 • Closed Nov–Apr • €€*

Left **Plage du Loto** Right **Ceramic ware on display in a workshop, Pigna**

Bastia and the North

WITH ITS RUGGED INTERIOR AND TURQUOISE WATER-*fringed coastline, the far north of Corsica, stretching from Bastia to Calvi via Cap Corse, confirms most of the clichés usually applied to the island. There is barely a patch of flat ground in the entire region. Journeys tend to be winding and take longer than you expect but reveal astonishing landscapes at every bend.*

The Italian influence is slightly more marked in the north too, especially around Bastia, whose Genoese-built Vieux Port could have been transported in its entirety from the Tuscan coast, visible on clear days across the Tyrrhenian Sea. The Genoese were also responsible for the most striking man-made landmark of the far north: Calvi's Citadelle, whose ochre walls preside over a magnificent panorama of sea and granite mountains.

Rue Notre Dame, the Citadelle, Bastia

Sights

1. Bastia
2. Cap Corse
3. Erbalunga
4. St-Florent
5. Pigna
6. L'Île Rousse
7. Calvi
8. Sant'Antonino
9. Patrimonio
10. Giunssani

Preceding pages **A small beach at Capo Pertusato**

Bastia

Bastia is the island's main centre of commerce and culture. Despite the fact that Napoleon appointed his home town Ajaccio as the official capital, Bastia has a more citified atmosphere than its rival. For visitors, the Vieux Port district of Terra Nova and the Citadelle overlooking it form the principal focus, and the Second Empire thoroughfares across town offer plenty of stylish places to shop (see pp18–19).

Cap Corse

Plunging sheer into the sea, the western flank of the Cap Corse peninsula is steep and relatively inhospitable, with schist-roofed hamlets clinging to the few balconies of level land above tiny harbours. The eastern side, however, has a gentler feel. Terraced vineyards, founded five centuries ago by the Genoese, cascade to a slither of undulating shoreline. It takes a day to round the cape by car, an experience not to be missed (see pp20–21).

Erbalunga

Only 9 km (6 miles) north of Bastia, the fishing port of Erbalunga (see p20) has almost become a suburb of the city – albeit one with a distinct identity

Erbalunga's promontory

of its own. The picturesque harbour's entrance is guarded by a stalwart watchtower and the Le Pirate restaurant (see p99) nearby serves excellent seafood. Erbalunga is also known across the island for its sombre Good Friday procession of masked penitents, La Cerca (see p42).

St-Florent

The absence of a white-sand beach within easy driving distance of the town has left the cluster of slate-tiled fishermen's houses packed around St-Florent's Citadelle delightfully unspoilt. There are some magnificent beaches across the gulf, such as the Plage du Loto, but you have to jump on a boat to get to them. The waterfront, lined with cafés, is truly atmospheric at sunset, when the Tenda hills behind turn molten red (see pp22–3).

View of the Citadelle, Bastia

5 Pigna

The sky-blue woodwork and immaculately pointed masonry testify to Pigna's government-funded renaissance as a centre for local arts and crafts. A dozen or more studios operate here, selling ceramics, musical boxes, bamboo flutes and Corsican citterns, among other things. Pigna's main hotel-restaurant, Casa Musicale *(see p99)* is a major centre for traditional Balagne music. ✆ *Map C4*

6 L'Île Rousse

Founded by Pascal Paoli midway along the Balagne coast in 1765, L'Île Rousse has thrived ever since, particularly after its rebirth as a French Riviera-style resort. The red isle from which the town derives its name rises to the north and a superb view extends from the lighthouse crowning it across the rooftops to the hills beyond. ✆ *Map C4*

Boats moored at Calvi marina

7 Calvi

Calvi's spectacular setting has lured visitors since the early days of tourism in the Mediterranean. Its attractions include a glamorous marina, a handful of baroque churches and the house claimed locally to be the birthplace of Christopher Columbus. The highlight of any visit is the glorious vision of the Genoese Citadelle, framed by its backdrop of brilliant blue sea and distant mountains *(see pp24–5)*.

8 Sant'Antonino

The constellation of pastel-washed, orange- and pink-granite villages strewn over the hillsides immediately inland from L'Île

View of L'Île Rousse at sunset

Rousse and Calvi, an area known as the Balagne, rank among the prettiest in the Mediterranean; and Sant'Antonino is widely regarded as the most picturesque of them all. Its warren of narrow, cobbled alleyways crowd like a bird's nest on the conical summit of a hill surveying a dramatic spread of sea and hills. ✎ *Map C4*

Patrimonio
The Genoese exported vast quantities of wine from Patrimonio – mostly the sweet, blossom-scented muscat with which the peninsula has since become synonymous. Today, however, only a few thousand hectares remain under cultivation, the bulk of them in the leeward side of Patrimonio's striking chalk escarpments. In the shadow of the village church, numerous wine caves offer tastings *(see p21)*.

A vineyard in Patrimonio

Giunssani
Given its proximity to the Balagne coast, it is amazing how few visitors venture into the beautiful Giunssani region, just over the mountain from L'Île Rousse. A hidden Shangri-la of pristine chestnut and pine forest, crashing streams and wonderful scenery, the region is dominated by the awesome profile of the 2,393-m (7,850-ft) high Monte Padro to the south. ✎ *Map C5*

The Cap Corse Corniche

Morning

🕐 A circuit of the Corniche can be completed in a full day. If you are troubled by local driving styles and the dizzying drops, follow it in a clockwise direction, ensuring you stay on the landward side of the road. Begin by heading out of **Bastia** *(see pp18–19)* on the D81, which crosses the ridge at windswept Col de Teghime, where a marvellous view over the Nebbio and bay is revealed. Stop for a coffee and croissant on the **Place des Portes** *(see p22)* in **St-Florent** *(see pp22–3)*, then proceed northwards through the vineyards of **Patrimonio** towards **Nonza** *(see p21)*, whose Genoese watchtower affords another stupendous view – this time west over the bay to the Désert des Agriates coast. The shoreline grows noticeably wilder as you press north. Pause at pretty **Centuri Port** *(see p21)* for a stroll around its little lobster-fishing harbour, then begin the zigzagging ascent of the Cap's northern tip to reach Barcaggio via the D253. Stop for lunch at the **U Fanale** restaurant *(see p99)*.

Afternoon

From Barcaggio, continue west to **Macinaggio** *(see p20)*, from where excursion boats run up the wild coastline further north. The remaining leg down the east coast of the Cap is an easier drive; be sure to stock up on fine muscat at the **Domaine Pieretti** vineyard en route *(see p63)*.

Left **Tour de Sénèque** Centre **An aubergine growing at Jardins Traditionnels** Right **Macinaggio**

TOP 10 Best of the Rest

1 Jardins Traditionnels du Cap Corse
Chronic depopulation has seen many of the edible plant species of Cap Corse disappear over the centuries. A cross section of them is preserved here *(see p21)*.

2 A Mimoria di u Vinu
This small community-run museum on the eastern cape near Luri showcases the region's wine industry, now enjoying something of a revival. *Place San Petru, Luri* ✆ *Map E2 • 04953 50644 • Open 10am–noon & 4–7pm Tue–Sat • Adm*

3 Tour de Sénèque
Crowning the Cap Corse watershed, this remote tower makes a fine vantage point over the northern cape *(see p20)*.

4 Boat Trip from Macinaggio
This 2-hour trip cruises past the Îles Finnachiarola bird colony, making swimming stops en route. ✆ *San Paulu, Port de Plaisance, Macinaggio • Map F1 • 04953 50709 • Boats depart at 11am • www.sanpaulu.com • Adm*

5 Plage de l'Ostriconi
This bay is a sweep of honey-coloured sand and jade-green water at the north-western edge of the Désert des Agriates. There's no café, so bring your own supplies. ✆ *Map C3*

6 Lama
As its grand period houses underline, Lama formerly ranked among the Balagne's most prosperous villages. It is now a sleepy backwater albeit a very pretty one. It also boasts its own open-air pool. ✆ *Map D4 • 04954 82404 • Pool open Jul & Aug • Adm*

7 Algajola
Packed around the western end of a broad, sandy beach, the village of Algajola numbers among Corsica's pleasant low-key seaside resorts. ✆ *Map C4*

8 Spel007cato
Extending to the distant sea, the view over the pale terracotta rooftops of Speloncato is one of the most famous in the Balagne region. ✆ *Map C4*

9 Vallée du Fango
The most grand of all the valleys cutting into Corsica's interior from the Balagne coast, Fango comes to an abrupt end at Paglia Orba's implacable north face. ✆ *Map B6*

10 Galéria
The final outpost of the Balagne before the coast road begins its long climb to the Col de la Palmarella and Golfe de Porto, this remote fishing village lies near several quiet beaches. ✆ *Map B5*

Left **A Casarella**

Price Categories

For a three-course meal for one with half a bottle of wine (or equivalent meal), taxes and extra charges.

€ under €20
€€ €20–€30
€€€ €30–€40
€€€€ €40–€50
€€€€€ over €50

⁀10 Places to Eat

1 Table du Marché
This smart terrace restaurant on Bastia's splendid 18th-century market square is the place to try fresh local delicacies. ✎ *Place du Marché, Bastia • Map P5 • 04953 16425 • Closed Sun • €€€€€*

2 A Casarella
Swordfish steaks, in flaky pastry with aubergine and mint, are the speciality of this restaurant in Bastia's Citadelle. ✎ *Rue Ste-Croix, Citadelle, Terra Nova, Bastia • Map P7 • 04953 20232 • Closed Mon lunch and Nov • €€€*

3 Le Pirate
The last word in gourmet Corsican seafood, Le Pirate also has a wine list second to none, served in style beside a lovely fishing harbour. ✎ *Erbalunga, 12 km north of Bastia • Map F3 • 04953 32420 • Open Mar–Dec • €€€€€*

4 U Fanale
With a more inspiring menu than most at the far northern end of the Cap, U Fanale has a perfect water's edge location. Try the grouper curry with apple sauce. ✎ *Barcaggio, Cap Corse • Map E1 • 04953 56272 • Open Apr–Nov • €€€*

5 Ferme-Auberge Campo di Monte
Enjoy veal ragout and courgette fritters at this farmhouse hidden on a remote Nebbio mountainside. Reservations are essential. ✎ *Murato • Map E4 • 04953 76439 • Open mid-Jun–mid-Sep • €€€€*

6 Casa Musicale
A convivial atmosphere prevails at this colourful restaurant in the Balagne. Most of the ingredients used to prepare the food are organic and locally sourced. ✎ *Place de l'Eglise, Pigna, Balagne • Map C4 • 04956 17731 • Closed Jan–mid-Feb • €€€ • www.casa-musicale.org*

7 L'Oggi
Perched high above the Golfe de Calvi in Lumio, this glitzy hotel-restaurant boasts a menu as exotic as the views. ✎ *Hôtel Chez Charles, Lumio • Map B4 • 04956 06171 • €€€€€*

8 L'Escale
Fresh Corsican mussels in Cap Corse liqueur number among the house specialities of this bustling, good-value eatery in the old quarter of L'Île Rousse. ✎ *Rue Notre Dame, L'Île Rousse. • Map C4 • 04956 01053 • Open Apr–mid-Oct • €€€€*

9 Le Pasquale Paoli
This is one of the few restaurants in Corsica to have garnered a Michelin star for its combination of traditional local flavours. ✎ *2 Place Paoli, L'Île Rousse • Map C4 • 04954 76770 • Closed Jan–Feb • €€€€€*

10 Campu Latinu
Dine alfresco under the oaks on the stone terraces of this charming restaurant, overlooking the pretty village of Lama. Their "menu corse" is great value. ✎ *Campu Latinu, Lama • Map D4 • 04954 82383 • Open daily • €€€*

STREETSMART

CORSICA'S TOP 10

Left **Euro currency** Centre **Holidaymakers, Porto-Pollo beach** Right **European electrical adaptor**

🔟 Planning Your Trip

1 When to Go

July and August are peak season in Corsica. Temperatures reach their hottest at this time, and during high season the beaches and resorts can get very crowded, and prices soar. A far more relaxing time to visit, both in terms of climate and visitor numbers, is May–early June and mid-September–mid-October.

2 What to Pack

Light summer clothes will suffice during peak season, but even then, a lightweight fleece or shawl may come in handy for cool evenings. From mid-September through mid-June, an extra layer or two is essential, as is a waterproof coat if you plan to venture into the hills of the interior.

3 Weather

Corsica enjoys classic Mediterranean weather: warm, dry and sunny from June till September, with temperatures reaching an average of nearly 30°C (86°F). In May and September, temperatures hover around 20–25°C (68–77°F). Rainfall is highest in October and November, although sudden storms can blow in at any time of the year.

4 Passports and Visas

No visa is required for EU nationals to visit France. Citizens of the US, Canada, Australia, New Zealand and Israel are permitted to visit for a maximum of three months without a visa. Everyone, however, is required to carry some form of identification on them at all times, which for visitors means a copy of their passport.
🌐 www.diplomatie.gouv.fr

5 Insurance

It is a good idea to obtain comprehensive travel insurance that covers health and personal belongings before going to Corsica. EU citizens carrying a European Health Insurance Card (EHIC) are entitled to reimbursement of most of the cost of state-provided medical treatment. Do not forget to take your insurer's emergency telephone number with you.
🌐 www.ehic.org.uk

6 Customs Regulations

There is no limit on goods that can be taken into or out of France for visitors from most EU countries. Travellers from outside the EU face heavier restrictions but, unlike EU citizens, are entitled to a limited amount of duty-free purchases.

7 Currency

Corsica uses the euro, for which bank notes are issued in denominations of 5 (grey), 10 (pink), 20 (blue), 50 (orange), 100 (green), 200 (yellow) and 500 (purple). The euro has eight coin denominations, ranging from €2 down to 1 cent.

8 Electricity

Electrical current in Corsica is 220v/50Hz AC. Except in older properties, the central hole of the sockets is generally earthed. Travellers from the UK and North America will need standard round-pin adapters, sold at most airports.

9 Special Equipment

If you are planning to do a lot of walking, a pair of lightweight, telescopic trekking poles is a sound investment, as are a pair of fins, a face mask and snorkel for days on the beach. Mats, parasols and other beach essentials are available in local supermarkets.

10 Time Zone

Corsica follows Central European time: one hour ahead of Greenwich Mean Time (GMT). Daylight saving time (DST) starts at 3am on the last Sunday in March and finishes at 2am on the final Sunday of October.

Left **easyJet service to Ajaccio** Centre **Local bus** Right **L'Île Rousse railway station**

🔟 Getting There and Around

1 Scheduled Flights

Air France and its subsidiary carrier CCM operate scheduled flights to Corsica from mainland France, with direct services from Paris, Marseille, Nice, Bordeaux, Toulouse and Lyon. Scheduled flights from the UK involve at least one change, usually in Paris or at a Riviera airport, and are more expensive than travelling with a low-cost carrier or charter.
✎ www.airfrance.com; www.aircorsica.com

2 Charter and Low-Cost Flights

easyJet flies to both Ajaccio and Bastia from various airports in the UK, and from other European cities. Charter fares are available through companies such as Holiday Options in the UK. Book well in advance for good deals. ✎ www.easyjet. com; www.ryanair.com

3 Airports

Corsica has four airports handling inter-national and domestic flights. Ajaccio (Campo dell'Oro) and Bastia (Poretta) are the busiest, followed by Calvi (Ste-Catherine) and Figari (Corse-du-Sud). Shuttle buses run from the first two, but from the others you will have to catch a cab into town.
✎ www.2a.cci.fr; www. bastia.aeroport.fr; www. calvi.aeroport.fr

4 Ferries

Ferries sail from many ports on the French and Italian Rivieras, and from neighbouring islands. Services to Ajaccio and Bastia from Nice, Toulon and Marseille are most frequent, but you can also catch boats to L'Île Rousse in the north and Propriano and Porto-Vecchio in the south ✎ www.corsicaferries.com; www.mobylines.com; www. saremar.it; www.sncm.fr

5 Car Hire

Avis, Hertz, Europcar and Citer have outlets across the island, including at the airports. Rates range from €280–€350 per week. Car seats for kids cost extra. Note that queues at the airport can get long when a flight arrives so head straight to a rental desk once you've reclaimed your baggage. ✎ www. avis.fr; www.hertzcorse. com; www.europcar.fr; www.citer.fr

6 Trains

Small local trains connect the towns of Ajaccio, Bastia, Corte, Calvi and L'Île Rousse. Call 04953 28057 for train times, or visit www.train-corse.com. Tickets can be purchased in advance at the station or online at the SNCF website. ✎ www.ter-sncf.com

7 Buses

Corsica's bus network is privately run by a variety of different firms and is not very well integrated. While services between major towns are frequent enough, those to outlying regions are often designed to coincide with school timetables and thus may not depart at convenient times.

8 Timetables

Timetables for all bus and train services can be obtained from tourist information offices. The Corsica bus website has interactive maps and useful tips for travelling on public transport around the island (in English and French).
✎ www.corsicabus.org

9 Walking

Walking is a great way to get around Corsica. Long-distance footpaths, impeccably waymarked and supported by a network of hostels, crisscross the island from coast to coast via its scenic highlights. Hiking can be a lot cheaper than other ways of getting around.

10 Off-Season Travel

All public transport to and from Corsica is drastically scaled back between mid-October and Easter. Only skeleton ferry services sail from the continent, and many bus routes are suspended altogether. Timetables for off-season services are available online. ✎ www. corsicabus.org

Left **Tourist information office, Macinaggio** Centre **Visitors with a map** Right **National Park logo**

🔟 Useful Information

1 Tourist Information

Most towns and large villages in Corsica have tourist information offices with English-speaking staff. Opening hours vary according to the time of year, but during the peak season the largest offices in Ajaccio and Bastia are usually open from 8am until 7pm Mon–Sat and from 9am until 1pm Sun.
🌐 *www.visit-corsica.com; www.ajaccio-tourisme.com; www.bastia-tourisme.com*

2 Parc Naturel Régional de Corse

Created in 1972, the Parc Naturel Régional de Corse (PNRC) protects nearly 40 per cent of the island's interior wilderness. Part of its job is to maintain Corsica's 1,500-km (932-mile) footpath network. Walkers often stop by the PNRC's office in Ajaccio for advice before setting off on a trek.
🌐 *Maison d'Information du PNRC, 2 Rue Major Lambroschini, Ajaccio • 04955 17910 • Open 8am–noon & 2–6pm Mon–Fri • www.parc-corse.org*

3 Websites

Corsica Isula (www. corsica-isula.com) is a detailed English-language site featuring lots of background on Corsica's culture, history and sights. For long-distance walkers, http//:corsica. forhikers.com is a useful source of online advice.

4 Opening Hours

Opening hours of shops and banks are typically 8:30/9am–1/1:30pm and 2:30/3–6/7pm, though these vary according to the business in question. Opening hours for museums, tourist offices and other visitor attractions change according to the season.

5 Consulates and Embassies

The nearest foreign consulates are on the mainland in Marseille. They will rarely intervene in legal matters but can provide support in the event of a grave emergency or a death.

6 Smoking

Smoking has officially been prohibited in all public places, including cafés, restaurants, cinemas, stations and nightclubs, since 2008. The ban received widespread support on the French mainland, but is routinely flaunted in Corsica. Complaints about insensitive puffing are unlikely to receive a sympathetic response.

7 Tipping

Service Compris on your bill or receipt means that a service charge has already been levied. Otherwise, assume that a gratuity of about 10 per cent will be expected if you have received polite, prompt service in a restaurant.

8 Maps

Google coverage of Corsica is crisp down to 50 m (100 ft), and Streetview coverage is comprehensive, even in outlying areas. The best printed map is the yellow Michelin 1:200,000. Walkers may wish to invest in IGN's pricey TOPO 1:25,000 maps, covering their chosen routes. 🌐 *www.michelin. co.uk; www.ign.fr*

9 Toilets

Public toilets are few and far between in Corsica. You will have to order a coffee or mineral water for the privilege of using the facilities in cafés and restaurants.

10 Public Holidays

France observes 13 public holidays, when most shops, offices, banks, and museums are closed *(see box)*.

Public Holidays

- 1 January
- Good Friday
- Easter Sunday
- Easter Monday
- Ascension Day
- Pentecost
- 1 May (Labour Day)
- 8 May (VE Day)
- 14 July (Bastille Day)
- 15 August (Assumption of the Virgin Mary)
- 1 November (All Saints)
- 11 November (Armistice Day)
- 25 December (Christmas)

Left **Telephone card** Centre **ATM** Right **Post office sign**

🔟 Banking and Communications

Banks
Standard opening hours for banks in Corsica are 8am–noon and 2–5pm Mon–Fri. Nearly all big branches offer foreign currency exchange, as well as Automatic Teller Machine (ATM) facilities. Note that as elsewhere in France, entry is via security doors operated remotely by a cashier from inside the building.

ATMs
There are many ATMs in Corsica's main towns, where you will find them outside most banks and post offices. You can use your normal debit or credit card to withdraw cash, for which you will be charged a small commission by your home bank.

Debit and Credit Cards
Bank cards are the most convenient and cost-effective way to access your money and to pay for major goods and services while you are in Corsica. However, not all restaurants and shops accept them: check in advance.

Card Security
To ensure your first credit or debit card transaction in Corsica isn't declined (a security measure triggered by using the card in a different country), contact your bank to inform them of your travel plans. Also, take along a spare in case the main card is ever declined at an ATM.

Post Offices
Distinguished by their yellow-and-blue livery, post offices – *Postes* or PTTs – are found in all Corsican towns and cities, and many villages. In cities, they are open 8am–7pm Mon–Fri and 8am–noon Sat; in smaller towns, 9am–noon and 2–4:45pm Mon–Sat. Stamps are also sold at newsagents and tobacconists.

Internet Access
Many shops and cafés in Corsican towns offer Internet access, charging around €5 per hour for browsing. Upscale hotels also have free Wi-Fi for guests and are worth approaching if you wish to access the Internet in locations outside the main towns.

Mobile Phones
Your mobile network supplier's French partner will automatically establish a local connection as soon as you first switch on your handset in Corsica. Coverage is sufficient in all but a handful of black spots in the interior, though you may struggle to get a signal high up in the mountains.

Public Telephones
Calls in public telephone booths may only be made using pre-paid cards *(cartes téléphoniqes prépayées)*, available at most newsagents on the island, in a range of denominations. Charges work out considerably lower than for most pay-as-you-go mobile phones registered abroad.

Dialling Codes
Corsica's ten-digit telephone numbers should be dialled in full when phoning from within the island or mainland France. From abroad, dial 00 (the international dialling code) followed by 33 (the code for France), then the ten-digit number minus the first zero, thus: 0033 4951 23456.

Travellers' Cheques
Travellers' cheques, issued by banks and agencies such as Thomas Cook and American Express, may be exchanged for hard currency at most Corsican banks. It is prudent to take along a few large-denomination cheques in case of emergencies. You will be required to present your passport as proof of identity when cashing the cheques.

Left **Fire brigade vehicle** Centre **Hospital, Corte** Right **Pharmacy sign**

🔟 Security and Health

1 Emergencies
Dial 15 for an ambulance, 16 for the fire service *(pompiers)*, 17 for the police *(gendarmes)* and 04956 11395 for the Corsican mountain rescue *(secours montagne)*. All these numbers can be accessed free of charge by phoning 112 from your mobile. *"Au secours"* is the French phrase for "help".

2 Personal Security
The nationalist-paramilitary and mafia-related violence with which Corsica has been associated for decades rarely, if ever, affects outsiders. Incidences of muggings and rape are also rare. However, you should take the same common-sense precautions here as you would at home.

3 Theft
Theft of valuables from unlocked cars, hotel rooms and villas is no more prevalent in Corsica than in any other part of the Mediterranean, and it can be easily prevented by remembering to lock up after yourself. Special care, however, should be taken when leaving possessions on crowded beaches in the peak season.

4 Lost Property
Any lost property found in Corsica is generally handed over to the nearest police station *(gendarmerie)*. *"Je voudrais recupérer un objet égaré"* ("I would like to claim a lost item") is the phrase you'll need to get things moving. Take along your passport as proof of identity.

5 Hospitals
Corsica has well-equipped hospitals with accident and emergency facilities *(see box)*.

6 Pharmacies
Identifiable by their prominent green crosses (illuminated at night), pharmacies are ubiquitous in Corsica. They stock a wide range of medicines, including homeopathic remedies. EU citizens can redeem the cost of prescriptions from their home health authority.

7 Dentists
Modern dentistry is the norm in Corsica. Contact your holiday company representative or ask your hotel owner for advice on where to go. Costs are comparable with those charged by private practitioners in the UK.

8 Sea Hazards
Sea anemones are the main concern for swimmers. Their tiny brown spines snap off and become lodged under the skin if trodden upon or touched and can rapidly cause inflammation, so steer clear of them. The same applies to jellyfish: their sting can be painful for an hour or two.

9 Wild Boar and Snakes
Encounters with wild boar are inevitable if you do much forest walking, but are without risk unless you meet a mother with piglets, in which case back off as quietly and as quickly as possible. There are no poisonous snakes on the island, although the slim, white whip snake *(sarpu)* may bite if startled.

10 Women Travellers
Travelling in Corsica presents no particular challenges for women. Corsican men are very different from their wolf-whistling Italian cousins across the water and incidents of sexual harassment are rare – a consequence of the seriousness with which such insults are regarded by Corsicans themselves.

Hospital Numbers
- Ajaccio: 04952 99090
- Bastia: 04955 51111
- Calvi: 04956 51122
- Sartène: 04957 79500
- Bonifacio: 04957 39573
- Porto-Vecchio: 04957 00111
- Corte: 04954 50500

Left **Crowded beach in peak season** Right **Well-equipped hikers**

Things to Avoid

1 School Holidays

The annual summer holidays – or *grandes vacances* – herald a massive influx of around 1.3 million visitors to Corsica. As a result, in July and August the most popular beaches are noisy and crowded, the prices of even basic items are extortionate and roads are jam-packed with traffic.

2 Travelling on Sundays

With the exception of July and August, when opening hours are temporarily extended, Corsica falls silent on Sundays. All the shops, including the big supermarkets, close, making life particularly difficult for new arrivals by plane.

3 Running Out of Fuel

Filling stations are common enough along national highways and other main roads, but are disconcertingly thin on the ground when you are off the beaten track. Check your fuel gauge regularly, and remember that most garages, apart from those near the airports, close on Sundays.

4 Rush Hours

Rush hours only really affect Corsica's larger towns, where they can be very frustrating. Moreover, with workers returning home for their midday meal, rush hour tends to happen four times a day. Getting to and from popular beaches can prove a stop-and-start affair in peak season.

5 Running Out of Cash

In quieter parts of the island, where there are few ATMs, running out of cash can be an embarrassing inconvenience. It is a good idea to carry plenty of spare money. If you run out, check if the local post office dispenses cash.

6 Strikes

Industrial action is more common in France than the UK or US, and regularly brings whole areas of the island to a virtual standstill, noticeably at the height of the summer holidays. Fuel strikes and walkouts by airport staff are most likely to affect foreign travellers. Always check the current situation before departure.

7 Losing Your Passport

Losing your passport is an inconvenience to be avoided at all costs. Without one you will be prevented from leaving France without first obtaining replacement travel documents from the nearest consulate (in Marseille or Paris).

8 Locking Your Key in Your Hire Car

This is frustratingly easy to do with modern French cars, and can result in a hefty bill. Should you lock yourself out of your car, your hire company will insist on dispatching a representative by taxi, and will then charge you both the return fare from wherever you rented the vehicle and an administration fee.

9 Hiking Without Preparation

Every year, unwary walkers perish in the Corsican mountains after venturing into wilderness without adequate equipment or navigation skills. Always keep to the waymarked path *(sentier balisé)* and make sure you have enough food, water and warm, waterproof clothing to see you through a sudden change in weather.

10 Falling Out With Locals

Corsicans are notoriously quick to take offence, and tend to react to any perceived insult with disproportionate force. As driving styles are somewhat more flamboyant than in northern Europe and North America, the roads can prove a particular flashpoint. Bear in mind that a finger raised in anger will almost certainly result in confrontation.

Left **A souvenir shop in Ajaccio** Right **Street café**

🔟 Budget Tips

1 Reduced Admission
Most museums, galleries and monuments charge for admission, but offer reduced rates for children and senior citizens. Discounts are also available for students on production of a valid International Student Identity Card (ISIC). Family tickets are somewhat rare.

2 High Season and Low Season
Accommodation rates soar in high season, peaking from mid-July through August. Even prices in supermarkets are raised ahead of the *grandes vacances*. If you are on a tight budget come in shoulder season (May–mid-June and September –mid-October) when the weather is fine and prices more restrained.

3 Budget Stays
Comfortable lodges punctuate all the main long-distance hiking routes in Corsica. Beds are generally arranged in four- or six-person dorms, and tend to be offered as a half-board package including breakfast and an evening meal.

4 Self Catering
Self-catering holidays are the norm in Corsica, where the bulk of visitor accommodation is in rented villas, apartments and cottages. The cost of the property is typically €900–€2850 per week depending on the season. This may seem high but it can be spread between two or three families.

5 Eating Out
You wll soon rip through your budget if you eat out every night in Corsica. As with everything else on the island, prices are on the high side. However, most restaurants offer *menus fixe* (fixed-price menus), which invariably are better value for money than eating à la carte.

6 Cafés
The price of drinks and light snacks in cafés throughout the island is extremely high and it is easy to rack up large bills without intending to. By law, establishments have to post their rates next to the bar, so if you are unsure about tariffs, check there.

7 Picnics
There is no better way to keep those lunch bills low than eating alfresco in the beautiful Corsican countryside. The island is dotted with perfect picnic spots that form the ideal backdrop for simple feasts of local bread, cheese and charcuterie.

8 Pack Carefully
Forget an essential piece of clothing or equipment and you'll face an unpleasant shock when you try to replace it in Corsica. While most items are available locally, they tend to be considerably more expensive than back home, especially fashionable clothes, sunglasses and swimwear. Try the local hypermarket first.

9 Shops and Supermarkets
Due to increased transport and storage overheads, Corsican supermarkets typically charge around 20 per cent more than their counterparts on the continent, which can come as a shock to budget-conscious travellers. Regular convenience stores, however, are even pricier – although on Sundays they may be your only source of supplies.

10 Car Parking
Paying car parks is a relatively new phenomenon in Corsica, but one which has caught on fast, especially around the beaches, where you will have to shell out between 3 to 8 euros to leave your vehicle. One way around this is to park behind a beach café that offers complimentary parking, though if you do, be sure to stop by at least for a cup of coffee.

Left **Scuba divers kitting up** Centre **Camp site in the mountains** Right **Cycling in Cap Corse**

10 Specialist Holidays

1 Walking
Numerous firms in Corsica and on the French mainland offer specialist walking holidays. While some may only provide basic bed, board and route cards, others lay on qualified local mountain guides and full baggage transfer between stages. Before booking, ensure the proposed itinerary is within your physical capability. 🕲 www.corsicamadness.com

2 Rock Climbing
Local rock climbing guides have to pass stringent examinations to become fully accredited and insurable, which means their rates are high if you employ them on a daily basis. Most, however, can offer competitive packages online, bundling their services with suitably sited accommodation and catering. 🕲 www.xtremesud.com

3 Water Sports
It is a good idea for water sports enthusiasts to book a package deal through a specialist operator such as Mark Warner – one of several outfits that run sailing, windsurfing, water-skiing, kitesurfing and scuba diving holidays in Corsica. 🕲 www.markwarner.co.uk

4 Horse Riding
While most Corsican riding schools offer basic day- or half-day trips, they will arrange longer outings too, with nights spent in lodges or mountain refuges along the way. For the full-on equestrian adventure of a lifetime, splash out on a two-week traverse of the island.

5 Cycling
Working out which of Corsica's coast, forest and mountain roads have the smoothest surfaces, most manageable gradients, inspiring views and least traffic is a task best left to the experts. A dedicated cycling holiday operator will also arrange all your food and accommodation, as well as a support vehicle. 🕲 www.velo-corse.com

6 Botanical and Ornithological
Corsica in the springtime, when the maquis is in full flower, is a wildlife lover's dream, though knowing where, and when, to find the rarities requires specialist knowledge. UK-based Nature Trek is among the few dedicated operators in this field, and offers an inspirational eight-day holiday based at various locations. 🕲 www. naturetrek.co.uk

7 Diving
Any of the numerous diving schools operating in Corsica offer package deals that cover escorted dives, accommodation and meals in a single price. This tends to work out better value than making your own arrangements. Pick firms at different ends of the island if you are visiting for two weeks or more. 🕲 www.stareso.com

8 Camping
Because of the weight restrictions on economy flights to Corsica, camping isn't a realistic option for most air travellers. The camping kit would exceed the 20-kg (44-lb) allowance. One solution is to book with Eurocamp which has a site with tents already set up on the east coast. 🕲 www. eurocamp.co.uk

9 Cultural
Corsicans are proud of their heritage – whether architectural, musical, linguistic or gastronomic – and a holiday based around the island's cultural riches would be a most rewarding one. Devise an itinerary yourself using this guide book, or get a tour operator to draw one up for you.

10 Bespoke
A tailor-made tour can be expensive, but is worthwhile if you are looking for a specialized itinerary. Using the advice of local experts, bespoke tours cover anything, from churches and prehistoric monuments to something more esoteric.

Left **Chambres d'hôtes** Centre **Refuge for hikers** Right **Camp site**

🔟 Accommodation Tips

1 Rental Accommodation

Strict environmental laws in Corsica limit construc-tion near the coastline. Hence, accommodation is in rented houses – primarily purpose-built villas with pools. The more pricey the villas, the more chic are the interiors and extensive the views. The best villas are block booked by holiday companies. 🅢 *Simpson Travel, Boat Race House, 61-67 Mortlake, High Street, London SW114 8HL, UK* • *+44 020 8392 5858* • *www.simpsontravel.com*

2 Hotels

Corsica has hotels to suit every pocket, ranging from inexpensive guest-houses with shared shower-toilets to chic boutique hotels boasting designer decor and dreamy overflow pools. Well-known chains such as Best Western and Logis de France are also well represented, mostly in the main towns.

3 Chambres d'Hôtes

The French equivalent of "bed and breakfast", chambres d'hôtes are rooms attached to family homes. Warm hospitality is the norm. Rooms are nearly always *en suite*, and the breakfasts are enormous. Evening meals are sometimes offered, especially in remote areas. 🅢 *04951 00614* • *www.gites-corsica.com*

4 Ferme-Auberges

An accommodation option offering rustic character and fine Corsican cooking is the *ferme-auberge* (farm inn). The highlight of such places is the food and location. The rooms are spacious and *en suite*. 🅢 *01535 71150* • *www. bienvenue-a-la-ferme.com*

5 Gîtes d'Étape and Refuges

Corsica's long-distance hiking routes are all served by *gîtes d'étape* (for the coast-to-coast paths) and mountain refuges (on the GR20). The former offer bunks in four- to six-bed dorms; rates usually include obligatory half board. Refuges are much more basic and may be booked in advance through the PNRC's website *(see p104)*.

6 Camp Sites

Most Corsican camp sites are equipped to the highest standards and are situated in great locations. They can get terribly cramped in peak season, but for the rest of the year offer relaxing places to pitch a tent. 🅢 *www.campingcorse.com*

7 Half Board

Half-board *(demi-pension)* rates cover bed, breakfast and evening meal. How good a deal this might be depends on the quality of accommodation and food

on offer, but it is usually a dependable way to keep costs down. Note that some places (particularly *gîtes d'étape*) levy obligatory half board in high season.

8 Hidden Extras

Beware the dreaded service charge slipped on the bottom of your hotel bill, which can bump it up by as much as 20 per cent, particularly at upscale hotels. The price charged for in-room phone use is also usually very high.

9 When to Book

Reserve as far in advance as possible for accommodation in peak season when most places become fully booked. In shoulder and low season, however, you may be tempted to defer booking to pick up good-value, late-availability discounts. Whatever time of the year you visit though, a deposit *(arrhes)* of 30 per cent usually has to be paid up front.

10 Disabled Travellers

Corsica still has some way to go when it comes to accessibility for wheelchair users. Many properties have only a few fully accessible rooms, and even those often lack roll-in-roll-out shower stalls. If you have special needs, mention them at the time of booking.

Price Categories

For a standard, double room per night (with breakfast if included), taxes and extra charges.

€	under €100
€€	€100–€250
€€€	€250–€350
€€€€	€350–€450
€€€€€	over €450

Left **Lobby area of La Signoria** Right **Room at the Palm Beach**

🔟 Luxury and Boutique Hotels

1 La Villa
A superb view over Calvi's Citadelle and bay is La Villa's highlight. A sleek, modern 5-star hotel offering rooms, suites or separate villas, it boasts no fewer than five pools, a spa and a Michelin-starred restaurant. ⊗ Chemin de Notre Dame de la Serra, Calvi • Map B4 • 0495 6 51010 • Closed mid-Nov–mid-Apr • www.hotel-lavilla.com • €€€€€

2 La Signoria
Festooned in citrus orchards and rose gardens, La Signoria is located about 4 km (3 miles) inland from Calvi, in a grand old farmhouse looking inland to the Balagne mountains. Oil paintings and distressed paint finishes set the tone of the interiors. ⊗ Route de la Forêt de Bonifatu, Calvi • Map B4 • 04956 59300 • Closed Jan–Mar • www.hotel-la-signoria.com • €€€€€

3 Palm Beach
The 10 luminous rooms of this boutique hotel enjoy extensive views over the Plage de Scudo to the Rive Sud. Its Michelin-starred restaurant (see p75) ranks among the best for seafood on the island. ⊗ Route des Sanguinaires, Ajaccio • Map H3 • 04955 20103 • www.palm-beach.fr • €€€€€

4 Le Maquis
Operating since the 1940s, Le Maquis ranks among Corsica's longest-established luxury hotels. Some find its hacienda-style interiors a little over-the-top, but the location is stunning and the restaurant (see p75) is top-notch. ⊗ BP 94, Porticcio • Map H3 • 04952 50555 • Closed Jan–Feb • www.lemaquis.com • €€€€€

5 Domaine de Murtoli
This fabulously remote private estate is ranged above an inaccessible cove on the Sartenais coast. It comprises a scattering of old, luxuriously refurbished farmhouses, with small pools, a gastronomic restaurant and liveried staff. ⊗ Sartène • Map J5 • 04957 16924 • www.murtoli.com • €€€€€

6 Les Maisons du Hameau Domaine Saparale
Set in the famed Saparale vineyards (see p62), these 19th-century guesthouses, made of antique wood and stone, each have their own hammam and outdoor pool. Rates are comparable with those of a luxury hotel, but there is more space and privacy. ⊗ 5 Cours Bonaparte, Sartène • Map K5 • 04957 71552 • Closed mid-Feb–mid-Mar • www.lehameaudesaparale.com • €€€€€

7 Casa del Mar
A red cedar and orange granite exterior contrasts with the chic designer interiors of this boutique hotel that overlooks the Golfe de Porto-Vecchio. The water-side location, pool and spa are a dream and the restaurant (see p83) is in a class of its own. ⊗ Route de Palombaggia, Porto-Vecchio • Map L5 • 04957 23434 • Closed Nov–mid-Apr • www.casadelmar.fr • €€€€€

8 Grand Hôtel de Cala Rossa
Driftwood furniture and teak decks mirror understated luxury in this exquisite hotel on the outskirts of Porto-Vecchio. It also boasts its own private beach, a spa, beach-side bar and Michelin-starred restaurant. ⊗ Cala Rossa, Porto-Vecchio • Map L5 • 04957 16151 • Closed Nov–mid-Apr • www.hotel-calarossa.com • €€€€€

9 Maison Rorqual
Built around outcrops of huge granite boulders on the rugged shoreline of the Désert des Agriates, Maison Rorqual consists of five luxury chalets, with sea views from their private patios. ⊗ Désert des Agriates, St-Florent • Map E3 • 04953 70537 • www.maison-rorqual.fr • €€€–€€€€€

10 U Palazzu Serena
Corsica's only art hotel occupies a beautifully restored 17th-century mansion on the edge of pretty Oletta village. Works by Anish Kapoor, Wendy Wischer and others adorn its nine rooms. ⊗ Paganacce, Oletta • Map E4 • 04953 83939 • www.upalazzuserenu.com • €€€–€€€€€

Rooms in all high-end hotels in Corsica come with air conditioning.

Left **Castel Brando** Right **Le Central**

Town Hotels

Le Central
Just off Bastia's Place St-Nicolas, Le Central has smart and homely furnishings, friendly management and is well maintained, ensuring it ranks among the best-value mid-range hotels on the island. ✦ *3 Rue Miot, Bastia • Map N5 • 04953 16972 • www.centralhotel.fr • €*

Les Voyageurs
With quirkily themed rooms ("Indians", "Jules Verne", "Cinema", etc), this family-run hotel in central Bastia possesses an idiosyncratic charm. It offers 3-star comforts at reasonable prices. ✦ *9 Av Maréchal Sebastiani, Bastia • Map N4 • 04953 49080 • www.hotel-lesvoyageurs. com • €€*

Castel Brando
The colour-washed walls, shuttered windows, rustic schist roofs and palm-filled garden lend elegance to this 19th-century mansion. The vaulted interiors are filled with antiques and there is an outdoor pool to lounge by. ✦ *Erbalunga, Cap Corse • Map F3 • 04953 01030 • Open Apr–Oct • www. castelbrando.com • €€*

Le Magnolia
This *belle époque*-style hotel is housed in a 19th-century residence just behind Calvi's Quai Landry. Le Magnolia derives its name from the 100-year-old tree in its courtyard. The terrace restaurant does a brisk trade in local cuisine. ✦ *Rue Alsace Lorraine, Calvi • Map B4 • 04956 51916 • Open Apr–Oct • www.hotel-le-magnolia. com • €€*

Hotel Santa Maria
The perfect place to stay in L'Île Rousse, Hotel Santa Maria has direct access to an adjacent beach. The rooms are comfortably furnished and some have sea-facing balconies. ✦ *Route du Porto, L'Île Rousse • Map C4 • 04956 30505 • www.hotel santamaria.com • €€*

Le Kallisté
This hotel fuses Napoleonic-era architecture with stylish modern fittings and furnishings to great effect. It enjoys a superb location in Ajaccio, with the Cours Napoléon literally on its doorstep. ✦ *51 Cours Napoléon, Ajaccio • Map P1 • 04955 13445 • www.hotel-kalliste-ajaccio.com • €€*

Les Mouettes
A luxurious hotel, Les Mouettes dates from Ajaccio's 19th-century heyday, and is in a splendid location on the Route des Sanguinnaires, looking straight across the gulf. It offers all the swank and modern conveniences you would expect from a 4-star hotel. ✦ *9 Cours Lucien Bonaparte, Ajaccio • Map N3 • 04955 04040 • Open Apr–mid-Nov • www. hotellesmouettes.fr • €€*

San Damianu
A smart, Swiss-run hotel on a natural balcony overlooking Sartène's medieval roofscape and Rizzanese Valley, San Damianu is the nicest place to stay in town. The decor is contemporary and rooms boast their own private terraces. ✦ *Quartier San Damien, Sartène • Map J5 • 04957 05541 • Open Apr–Oct • www.sandamianu.fr • €€*

Centre Nautique
Sea-weary sailors alighting on the adjacent quayside form the mainstay of this waterfront boutique hotel, which, thanks to its location and gorgeous wood decor, rivals Le Genovese as the finest luxury option in Bonifacio. ✦ *Quai Nord, Bonifacio • Map K7 • 04957 30211 • Open May–Oct • www. centre-nautique.com • €€*

Le Genovese
This 5-star hotel overlooks Bonifacio's port from a ledge beside the Citadelle walls. The earthy interiors open on to a secluded courtyard and pool, lit up by candles and lanterns at night. ✦ *Haute Ville, Bonifacio • Map K7 • 04957 31234 • Open Jan–Oct • www.hotel-genovese.com • €€€€*

Price Categories

For a standard, double room per night (with breakfast if included), taxes and extra charges.

€ under €100
€€ €100–€250
€€€ €250–€350
€€€€ €350–€450
€€€€€ over €450

Left **Exterior of La Roya with a view of the pool**

🔟 Seaside Hotels

1 Pietracap
Located 3 km (2 miles) north of Bastia, this 3-star hotel boasts rooms with water-facing balconies overlooking the Tyrrhenian Sea. There is also a pool and private access to a pebble beach. ✆ 20 Route de San Martino, Pietranera • 04953 16463 • Open Apr–Nov • www.hotel-pietracap. com • €€

2 La Roya
The rooms in this waterfront hotel near St-Florent are pleasantly furnished, the garden tumbles right down to the sand and the restaurant boasts a coveted Michelin star. ✆ Plage de la Roya, St-Florent • Map E3 • 04953 70040 • Open mid-Apr–mid-Nov • www. hoteldelaroya.com • €€€€

3 Les Roches Rouges
A historic hotel on the outskirts of Piana, Les Roches Rouges has altered little since it was originally built in 1912. The sea-facing rooms are simple but their windows open to a breathtaking view over the Calanches and Golfe de Porto. ✆ Piana • Map A7 • 04952 78181 • Open mid-March–mid-Nov • www.lesroches rouges.com • €€

4 U Capu Biancu
A chic, secluded 4-star hotel up the coast from Bonifacio, U Capu Biancu has idyllic bay views from its 39 rooms and a pool. The grounds, studded with granite boulders, adjoin two private beaches, one of which has an exclusive bar-restaurant. ✆ Route Canetto, Santa Manza, Bonifacio • Map K7 • 04957 30558 • Open May–mid-Oct • www.ucapu biancu. com • €€€€

5 Le Lido
Positioned on a rocky promontory at the entrance to Propriano's harbour, Le Lido stands just above the water, surveying a gentle curve of white sand. ✆ Av Napoléon, Propriano • Map J5 • 04957 60637 • Open mid-Apr–Sep • www.le-lido. com • €€€

6 Lilium Maris
This modern, simply furnished 3-star hotel on the water's edge overlooks the magnificent Tizzano beach. The hotel is well placed for explorations on foot of the Sartenais coast's least frequented stretches. ✆ Plage de Tizzano, Sartène • Map J6 • 04957 71220 • Open late-Mar–early Nov • www.lilium-maris.com • €€

7 Les Bergeries de Palombaggia
Local granite and terracotta tiles dominate the exterior of this rustic-chic boutique hotel near Porto-Vecchio. The wood balconies, poolside deck, overflow pool and terraces offer a splendid view over a row of umbrella pines to one of the Mediterranean's loveliest beaches. ✆ Porto-Vecchio • Map L6 • 04957 00323 • Open mid-Apr–mid-Nov • www.hotel-palombaggia.com • €€€€

8 Le Pinarello
Dominating the graceful arc of Pinarello beach, Le Pinarello may not look pretty from the outside, but the views from inside it, extending across the bay, are beautiful. The light-toned interiors are stylish. ✆ Plage de Pinarello, Sainte-Lucie-de-Porto-Vecchio • Map L4 • 00495 714439 • Open mid-Apr–mid-Oct • www. lepinarello.com • €€€€

9 La Solenzara
Located in a stately 17th-century Genoese mansion, La Solenzara's flower-filled grounds overlook the beach. The rooms retain a period feel. ✆ Quartier du Palais, Solenzara • Map L3 • 04955 74218 • Open mid-Mar–mid-Nov • www.hotel-lasolenzara. com • €€

10 Le Goéland
Elegance and simplicity are the watch-words of this family-run hotel in the Porto-Vecchio marina. A brief walk from the Cita-delle, it is central yet on the water. ✆ La Marine, Porto-Vecchio • Map L5 • 04957 01415 • Open mid-Mar–mid-Nov • www. hotelgoeland.com • €€€

Left **Hôtel des Touristes** Right **A Flatta, swimming pool**

🔟 Mountain Hotels

1 De la Poste
A 19th-century former coaching inn high in the hills of the Alta Rocca, De La Poste offers basic comforts (shared loos only) but lots of old-world charm. The rates are good value. ✆ Aullène • Map K4 • 04957 86121 • Open May–Sep • www.hotel-de-la-poste-aullene.com • €

2 Monte d'Oro
With its red-iron roofs, wax-polished wood floors and ceilings festooned with ivy creepers, the Monte d'Oro is redolent of the late 1800s. The rooms are old-fashioned but charming, and the dining room is a living museum. ✆ Vivario, Vizzavona • Map K1 • 04954 72106 • Open May–early Oct • www. monte-oro.com • €

3 Hôtel Des Touristes
Dating from 1928, this ski resort up in the Vallée de Niolo is a period hotel, little altered in decades. It is popular primarily with walkers. Do not miss breakfast in the fabulously straight-laced grande salle. ✆ Hôtel des Touristes, Calacuccia • Map C6 • 04954 80004 • Open May–Oct • www.hotel-des-touristes.com • €

4 Hôtel Dominique Colonna
Next to a mountain stream in the spectacular Vallée de la Restonica, this charming hotel is just the right place to relax next to the lovely pool, or the open fire at night. Good value. ✆ Vallée de la Restonica, Corte • Map D6 • 04954 52565 • Open mid-Apr–Oct • www.dominique-colonna.com • €€

5 A Flatta
A boutique hotel, hidden in the wild valley above Calenzana, A Flatta is known for its gourmet restaurant. It also offers a handful of pool-facing rooms with contemporary four-posters sporting exposed beams and gossamer drapes. ✆ Calenzana • Map B5 • 0495 6 28038 • Open May–Dec • www.aflatta.com • €€

6 Casa Musicale
Wake up to the tinkling of sheep's bells in this gem of a small hotel. From its dreamy rooms, painted in fresh Mediterranean colours, you can gaze through windows framed by fig trees to the distant Balagne coast. ✆ Pigna • Map C4 • 04956 17731 • Open mid-Mar–mid-Nov • www.casa-musicale.org • €

7 U Palazzu
This lovely heritage hotel in Pigna occupies a sensitively restored early-18th-century manor house on a hilltop surveying a glorious sweep of mountain and sea. The former seat of the Franchesini family, it is packed with heirlooms, and there is a superb terrace restaurant. ✆ Pigna • Map C4 • 04954 73278 • Open Apr–Oct • www.hotel-corse-palazzu.com • €€

8 Mare e Monti
Dating from 1870, this hotel occupies an old palace, with a belle époque reception salon that has retained its original oil portraits and gilt tapestries. There's also a luxurious pool and a garden restaurant. ✆ Feliceto • Map C4 • 04956 30200 • Open mid-Apr–mid-Oct • www.hotel-maremonti.com • €€

9 Auberge l'Aghjola
An attractive rural inn, Auberge l'Aghjola has stripped-wood floors, antique furniture and exposed beams in its rooms, most of which have fine views over the glorious Giunssani valley. Top-notch mountain cuisine is served in its dining hall. ✆ Pioggiola, Giunssani • Map C4 • 04956 19048 • Open Apr–Sep • www.aghjola.com • €€

10 Chez Pierrot
This guesthouse is legendary for its rustic hospitality, home-made charcuterie and the postprandial sing-alongs of the patron. Accommodation is in simple stone chalets and offers superb value. ✆ Chez Pierrot, Hameau de Jallicu. Jallicu, near Quenza, Alta Rocca • Map K4 • 04957 86321 • www.chez pierrot.over-blog.com • €

Price Categories

For a standard, double room per night (with breakfast if included), taxes and extra charges.

€	under €100
€€	€100–€250
€€€	€250–€350
€€€€	€350–€450
€€€€€	over €450

Left **Chez Gilles et Elise** Right **Casa Maria**

🔟 Bed & Breakfasts

1 Chateau Cagninacci

This aristocratic B&B, in a little-visited corner of Cap Corse, occupies an old Capucin convent – a rambling, mid-17th-century pile ranged around a central cloister. ⓢ San Martino di Lota, near Bastia • Map E3 • 06782 90394 • Open mid-May–Sep • www.chateau cagninacci.com • €€

2 Casa Maria

Located just off Nonza's square, Casa Maria's impeccably clean, tiled rooms look out from the gulf of St-Florent to the coast of the Désert des Agriates. Breakfast is served on a sun-dappled terrace. ⓢ Nonza, Cap Corse • Map E3 • 04953 78095 • Open Apr–Oct • www.casamaria-corse. com • €

3 Domaine de Crocano

This superb 18th-century farmhouse provides everything you could wish for from a Corsican B&B: views across rolling maquis and vineyards to the sea, fine dining, guided walks, horseback promenades and warm hospitality. ⓢ Route de Granace, near Sartène • Map J5 • 04957 71137 • Closed Dec • www. corsenature.com • €

4 Littariccia

Set amid a grove of olive trees on a hillside overlooking the Plage de Palombaggia, Littariccia is more like a boutique hotel than a B&B, with orange granite architecture and artfully styled, sea-facing rooms. ⓢ Route de Palombaggia, near Porto-Vecchio • Map L6 • 04957 04133 • Open Apr–Dec • www.littariccia. com • €€

5 La Diligence

A homely, inexpensive B&B, on the edge of one of Castagniccia's prettiest and most remote villages, La Diligence offers beautifully decorated rooms and sweeping views from its terrace over the chestnut canopy. The hosts also rustle up delicious local cuisine. ⓢ Verdèse, near Campana, Castagniccia • Map E6 • 04953 42633 • Open Apr–mid-Nov • €

6 Casa Capellini

A 1930s grocer's shop has been converted into this guesthouse of great charm. Its valley views are the great selling point, but the meals, prepared from local organic produce, get rave reviews too. ⓢ Sant'Andrea di Bozio, Bozio, near Corte • Map E7 • 04954 86933 • Open Apr–Oct • www.casacapellini. com • €

7 Chez Antoinette et Charles

This B&B, in a grand old Venachais house, doubles as a lodge for hikers. A lively, convivial atmosphere prevails on its terrace in summer. All four rooms are en suite and pleasantly furnished. ⓢ Saint Pierre de Vanaco • Map D7 • 04954 70729 • Open Apr–Sep • €

8 Chez Marie-Ange Ribeiro

B&Bs do not come more remote than this one, perched on the flank of a mountainside in the isolated Giunssani region. The building looks as old as the hills but has been made from scratch using reclaimed materials. ⓢ Olmi Capella, Giunssani • Map D5 • 04956 19101 • Open Apr–Oct • €

9 Chez Gilles et Elise

The sunny terrace of this pretty schist cottage looks down the valley and out to sea. The rooms, though small, are tastefully furnished and the breakfasts are copious. ⓢ Figarella and Miomo, Cap Corse • Map E3 • 04953 32565 • www. medori.net • €

10 L'Altu Pratu

On the outskirts of Bozio village, this modern house offers spacious, en suite rooms. There's a fair-sized pool and after dinner, the host regales guests with Corsican songs accompanied on mandolin and guitar. ⓢ Erbajola, Bozio, near Corte • Map E7 • 049 54 88007 • www. altupratu.com • €€

Left **U Monte Cintu** Centre **Le Bodri** Right **Camping Tuani**

Camp Sites

1 Sole e Vista
The most atmospheric of four large camp sites in the Spelunca Valley on the west coast, Sole e Vista's varied forest cover and irregular terracing retains the feel of a wild camp – though it has well-maintained sanitary blocks and a café. ✪ *Centre ville, Porto • Map B6 • 04952 61571 • Open Apr–Oct • www.camping-sole-e-vista.com*

2 U Stazzu
The rock-hard, sloping ground at this small site at the tip of Cap Corse will take its toll on your tent pegs, but it is located close to town and is only a five-minute walk from the nearest beach. It also runs a popular pizzeria in season. The rates are reasonable. ✪ *Route Acqua Salse, 1 km north of Macinaggio, Cap Corse • Map F1 • 04953 543 76• Open May–Oct • www. camping-u-stazzu.jimdo.com*

3 U Cavaddu Senza Nome
This wonderful site in the Vallée de l'Ortolo is spread out under cork trees and towering granite cliffs. It is run by a couple of German beekeepers and is perfect for kids. ✪ *Vallée de l'Ortolo, Sartene • Map K5 • 06103 91429 • Open May–Oct • www.ucavaddu.fr*

4 Corsica Camping
Corsica's first chain of campsites offers tours around this beautiful island

using a tent, camper or caravan (either yours or renting theirs). They also offer sites with bungalows, mobile homes and cute chalets. ✪ *04952 11447 • www.corsicacamping.com*

5 Arepos Roccapina
Brave the bone-jarring, 2.5-km (2-mile) drive down a rough track from the nearest main road, and the rewards are an inexpensive camp site behind an exquisite bay of powder-white sand and turquoise water. ✪ *Baie de Roccapina, Sartenais • Map J6 • 04957 71930 • Open May–Sep*

6 L'Albadu
This rustic farm, at a horse riding centre on the hillside overlooking Corte, has terrific views and first-rate facilities. There is always plenty of room but it is a bit of a trudge from the centre of town for those travelling by public transport. ✪ *Centre Equestre Albadu Pulicani, Ancienne Route d'Ajaccio, Corte • Map D6 • 04954 62455 • www. hebergement-albadu.fr*

7 Camping Tuani
For the full-on Restonica experience, camp under the 100-year-old pines beside a rushing mountain torrent where you can swim in deep, green pools. Close to the trail for Monte Rotondo, Camping Tuani makes the perfect base from which to embark on

walking adventures. ✪ *Vallée de la Restonica • Map D7 • 04954 61165 • Open mid-Apr–mid-Sep • www.campingtuani.com*

8 U Monte Cintu
You can almost reach out and touch the summit of Corsica's highest peak from the leafy terraces of this remote camp site, situated in a chestnut grove, on the elevated northern flank of the Vallée de Niolo. You can choose from among 80 sites. ✪ *Lozzi, Vallée de Niolo • Map C6 • 04954 80445 • Open mid-May–mid-Sep • www.camping-montecintu.com*

9 Camping d'Arone
A slick, professionally run site located a short walk away from a glorious beach of golden sand and blue water, and flanked by wild hillsides. It is busy in high season but at other times is a dream spot to hole up for a week or more. ✪ *Plage d'Arone, Piana • Map A7 • 04952 06454 • Open Mid-Apr–mid-Sep*

10 Le Bodri
A sprawling camp site, Le Bodri gets incredibly crowded in high summer but is virtually empty in shoulder season. It is right above a pair of divine little pearl-white beaches. ✪ *RN 197, Route de Calvi • Map C4 • 04956 01086 • Open May–Sep • www.campinglebodri.com*

The fees at all camp sites listed on this page are €15–€22 per night for two people, one tent and a car.

Left **Restaurant at Auberge du Col de Bavella** Right **Ustaria di a Rota**

🔟 Gîtes d'Étapes

L'Alzelli
This lodge features on the penultimate day of the Tra Mare e Monti Nord route along the west coast. Located in the middle of the mountains, next to a splendid river, it is a superb place to end a day's hiking. ⌾ *Tuarelli • Map B5 • 04956 20175 • Open Mid-Apr–mid-Oct*

A Funtana
Monte Estremo is the most remote location reachable by surfaced road in Corsica and the village *gîte* serves as a comfortable base for forays into the nearby wilderness. ⌾ *Monte Estremo, Manso, Vallée du Fango • Map B6 • 04953 43603, 04952 42166 • Open Apr–Oct*

Luna Piena
A privately run lodge on a high balcony, Luna Piena overlooks the eastern plain. It has 20 bunks and a welcoming "patron" and is intended mainly for walkers setting off (east to west) on the Mare a Mare trail, but anyone can stay here. ⌾ *Hameau Penti, Santa-Reparata-di-Moriani, East Coast • Map F6 • 04953 85948 • Open Apr–Oct*

La Cabane du Berger
There are two separate *gîtes* in Girolata. This one is the nicer of the two, with funky little wood cabins under the eucalyptus trees behind the beach and a water-front café. ⌾ *Girolata, Osani, West Coast • Map B6 • 04952 01698 • Open Apr–Sep*

U Poghju
This lodge has long enjoyed a strong reputation among Tra Mare e Monti Nord hikers for its spacious dorms and generous wood-grilled suppers, served alfresco in the garden. ⌾ *Capo Sottano, Évisa • Map B7 • 04952 62188 • Open Apr–Oct*

Ustaria di a Rota
Host Paul Ceccaldi's famous hospitality, which extends from excellent food to after-dinner songs, explains the near legendary status of this *gîte*-cum-refuge, high in the hinterland of Porto on the Mare a Mare Nord/Tra Mare e Monti trails. ⌾ *Marignana • Map B7 • 04952 62121*

Bella Vista
There are sunny, six-bed dorms with panoramic views over the Haut Taravo valley at this *gîte*. Host Baptiste Pantalacci brings a great sense of vocation to his role as warden and the meals his mother prepares, using his father's free-range charcuterie, are excellent. ⌾ *Cozzano, Haut Taravao, Corse-du-Sud • Map K3 • 04952 44159 • Open Apr–mid-Oct*

E Case
Run by the National Park Authority and half-an-hour's trek from Revinda, E Case occupies an old shepherd's hut where you can eat hearty mountain cooking and admire the gorgeous Mediterranean landscape from an ancient stone terrace. ⌾ *Parc Naturel Regional de Corse, Revinda, near Cargèse, West Coast • Map G1 • 04952 64819 • Open Apr–Sep*

U Cartalavonu
With its wonderful maritime pine forest and ghoulish boulder outcrops, the Massif de l'Ospédale *(see p81)* rising inland from Porto-Vecchio has its own distinct atmosphere. This well-run little *gîte* on the Mare a Mare Sud route oozes with local character, and has an open fire and lively bar. ⌾ *Ospédale, Corse-du-Sud • Map K5 • 04957 00039 • Open Apr–Sep*

Auberge du Col de Bavella
This superb lodge on the roadside below the Col de Bavella faces the famous Aiguilles de Bavella. Its wood-lined interior is filled with hiking, climbing and hunting memorablila. The hostel has its own self-catering kitchen and there is a cosy restaurant on site. ⌾ *Col de Bavella • Map L4 • 04957 20987 • Open Apr–mid-Nov*

The standard price for all gîtes d'étapes *listed on this page is €15–€18 per dorm bed or €35–€40 per person half board.*

General Index

Index

Acknowledgments

Photographer Tony Souter
Additional Photography Max Alexander, Fabrizio Ardito, Rough Guides/David Abram, Kathryn Tomasetti.
Fact Checker Catherine Gauthier

At DK INDIA
Managing Editor Aruna Ghose
Editorial Manager Sheeba Bhatnagar
Design Managers Kavita Saha, Mathew Kurien
Project Editor Vatsala Srivastava
Project Designer Neha Dhingra
Assistant Cartographic Manager Suresh Kumar
Cartographer Jasneet Kaur
Senior Picture Research Coordinator Taiyaba Khatoon
Picture Researcher Sumita Khatwani
Senior DTP Designer Azeem Siddiqui
DTP Designer Rakesh Pal
Indexer Andy Kulkarni
Proofreader Indira Chowfin

At DK LONDON
Publisher Vivien Antwi
List Manager Christine Stroyan
Senior Managing Art Editor Mabel Chan
Project Editors Rada Radojicic, Alexandra Whittleton
Designer Tracy Smith
Cartographer Stuart James
Picture Research Assistant Marta Bescos Sanchez
Senior DTP Designer Jason Little
Production Controller Mandy Inness

Revisions Team
Kate Berens, Niki Foreman, Michelle Arness Frederic, Bharti Karakoti, Claire Naylor, Susie Peachey, Ellen Root, Sophie Wright, Conrad Van Dyk

Picture Credits
Placement Key: a-above; b-below/bottom; c-centre; f-far; l-left; r-right; t-top.

Photography Permissions
Dorling Kindersley would like to thank the following for their assistance and kind permission to photograph at their establishments:

A Casarella, Ajaccio Cathedral, Auberge Santa Barbara, Castel Brando, L'Auberge du Col de Bavella, L'Oratoire de l'Immaculée Conception, L'Ortu, La Signoria, Le Central, Le Grand Cafe Napoleon, Les Roches Rouges, Musée de l'Alta Rocca, Musée de la Corse, Palm Beach, St-Jean-Baptiste.

Also all the other museums, hotels, restaurants, shops, galleries and other sights too numerous to thank individually.

The publisher would like to thank the following individuals, companies, and picture libraries for their kind permission to reproduce their photographs:

A PIGNATA: 60br, 61cl, 65cl.

ALAMY IMAGES: Christophe Boisvieux 42tl; Peter Bowater 40br; Eric Nathan 39tr.

CALVI ON THE ROCKS: Steve Wells – stevewells-photo.com 44tr, 44br, 45tr.

CASA MUSICALE: 64tr.

CORBIS: Christophe Boisvieux 51tr; Eye Ubiquitous / Bob Gibbons 87cl; Hemis / Georges Antoni 57cla / Pawel Wysocki 6cla; Hulton-Deutsch Collection 33cla, 33cr.

CORSICA MADNESS: 58tr.

DAVID COUTELLE: 90tl, 90tr.

DOMAINE DE MURTOLI: Camille Moirenc 49tr.

FESTIVAL DU FILM DE LAMA: Christophe Boisvieux 42tr, 42bl, 43tr, 43br.

MUSÉE DE LA CORSE: 32tl, 32tr, 33tr.

LES MUSICALES DE BASTIA: 45br.

NAVEVA: 52cla.

LE NUITS DE LA GUITARE: Frédéric Dupertuys 44cla, 45cr. OFFICE MUNICIPAL DE TOURISME D'AJACCIO: 43cla.

PALAIS FESCH MUSEE DES BEAUX ARTS/RMN: Gérard Blot 9cr, 10tr, 11br.

PHOTOLIBRARY: Age fotostock / JD. Dallet 94cr, / Jose Fuste Raga 16–17c, 34br, / Marevision Marevision 54tr, 55tr; Axiom / Paul Miles 89tl; Johner Bildbyra 109tc; Norbert Eisele-Hein 56bl; Iconotec 20–21c; Robert Harding Travel / Nelly Boyd 107tl / Yadid Levy 73tr, Peter Thompson 24–25c; White / Medio Images 100–101.

RESTAURANT LE PIRATE: 64br.

ROLAND HUITEL: 44tl.

WIKIPEDIA: 11cr.

All other images © Dorling Kindersley.
For further information see: www.dkimages.com.

Phrase Book

In Emergency

Help!	**Au secours!**	oh sekoor
Stop!	**Arrêtez!**	aret-ay
Call a doctor!	**Appelez un médecin!**	apuh-lay uñ medsañ
Call an ambulance!	**Appelez une ambulance!**	apuh-lay oon oñboo-loñs
Call the police!	**Appelez la police!**	apuh-lay lah poh-lees
Call the fire brigade!	**Appelez les pompiers!**	apuh-lay leh poñ-peeyay

Communication Essentials

Yes/No	**Oui/Non**	wee/noñ
Please	**S'il vous plaît**	seel voo play
Thank you	**Merci**	mer-see
Excuse me	**Excusez-moi**	exkoo-zay mwah
Hello	**Bonjour**	boñzhoor
Goodbye	**Au revoir**	oh ruh-vwar
Good night	**Bonsoir**	boñ-swar
What?	**Quel, quelle?**	kel, kel
When?	**Quand?**	koñ
Why?	**Pourquoi?**	poor-kwah
Where?	**Où?**	oo

Useful Phrases

How are you?	**Comment allez-vous?**	kom-moñ talay voo
Very well,	**Très bien**	treh byañ
Pleased to meet you.	**Enchanté de faire votre connaissance.**	oñshoñ-tay duh votr kon-ay-sans
Where is/are...?	**Où est/sont...?**	oo ay/soñ
Which way to...?	**Quelle est la direction pour...?**	kel ay lah deer-ek-syoñ poor
Do you speak English?	**Parlez-vous anglais?**	par-lay voo oñg-lay
I don't understand.	**Je ne comprends pas.**	zhuh nuh kom-proñ pah.
I'm sorry.	**Excusez-moi.**	exkoo-zay mwah

Useful Words

big	**grand**	groñ
small	**petit**	puh-tee
hot	**chaud**	show
cold	**froid**	frwah
good	**bon**	boñ
bad	**mauvais**	moh-veh
open	**ouvert**	oo-ver
closed	**fermé**	fer-meh
left	**gauche**	gohsh
right	**droit**	drwah
entrance	**l'entrée**	l'on-tray
exit	**la sortie**	sor-tee

Shopping

How much does this cost?	**C'est combien s'il vous plaît?**	say kom-byañ seel voo play
I would like...	**je voudrais...**	zhuh voo-dray
Do you have?	**Est-ce que vous avez?**	es-kuh voo zavay
Do you take credit cards?	**Est-ce que vous acceptez les cartes de crédit?**	es-kuh voo zaksept-ay leh kart duh kreh-dee
What time do you open?	**A quelle heure vous êtes ouvert?**	ah kel urr voo zet oo-ver
What time do you close?	**A quelle heure vous êtes fermé?**	ah kel urr voo zet fer-may
This one.	**Celui-ci.**	suhl-wee-see
That one.	**Celui-là.**	suhl-wee-lah
expensive	**cher**	shehr
cheap	**pas cher, bon marché**	pah shehr, boñ mar-shay
size, clothes	**la taille**	tye
size, shoes	**la pointure**	pwañ-tur
white	**blanc**	bloñ
black	**noir**	nwahr
red	**rouge**	roozh
yellow	**jaune**	zhohwn
green	**vert**	vehr
blue	**bleu**	bluh

Types of Shop

antique shop	**le magasin d'antiquités**	maga-zañ d'oñteekee-tay
bakery	**la boulangerie**	booloñ-zhuree
bank	**la banque**	boñk
bookshop	**la librairie**	lee-brehree
cake shop	**la pâtisserie**	patee-sree
cheese shop	**la fromagerie**	fromazh-ree
chemist	**la pharmacie**	farmah-see
department store	**le grand magasin**	groñ maga-zañ
delicatessen	**la charcuterie**	sharkoot-ree
gift shop	**le magasin de cadeaux**	maga-zañ duh kadoh
greengrocer	**le marchand de légumes**	mar-shoñ duh lay-goom
grocery	**l'alimentation**	alee-moñta-syoñ
market	**le marché**	marsh-ay
newsagent	**le magasin de journaux**	maga-zañ duh zhoor-no
post office	**la poste, le bureau de poste, le PTT**	pohst, booroh duh pohst, peh-teh-teh
supermarket	**le supermarché**	soo pehr-marshay
tobacconist	**le tabac**	tabah
travel agent	**l'agence de voyages**	l'azhoñs duh vwayazh

Sightseeing

abbey	**l'abbaye**	l'abay-ee
art gallery	**la galerie d'art**	galer-ree dart
bus station	**la gare routière**	gahr roo-tee-yehr
cathedral	**la cathédrale**	katay-dral
church	**l'église**	l'ayglees
garden	**le jardin**	zhar-dañ
library	**la bibliothèque**	beebleeo-tek
museum	**le musée**	moo-zay
railway station	**la gare (SNCF)**	gahr (es-en-say-ef)
tourist information office	**renseignements touristiques, le, syndicat d'initiative**	roñsayn-moñ tourees-teek sandee-ka d'eenee-syateev
town hall	**l'hôtel de ville**	l'ohtel duh veel

Staying in a Hotel

Do you have a vacant room?	**Est-ce que vous avez une chambre?**	es-kuh voo-zavay oon shambr

Phrase Book

double room, with double bed	**la chambre à deux personnes, avec un grand lit**	shambr ah duh pehr-son avek un gronñ lee
twin room	**la chambre à deux lits**	shambr ah duh lee
single room	**la chambre à une personne**	shambr ah oon pehr-son
room with a bath, shower	**la chambre avec salle de bains, une douche**	shambr avek sal duh bañ, oon doosh
I have a reservation.	**J'ai fait une réservation.**	zhay fay oon rayzehrva-syoñ

Eating Out

Have you got a table?	**Avez-vous une table de libre?**	avay-voo oon tabhl duh leebr
I want to reserve a table.	**Je voudrais réserver une table.**	zhuh voo-dray rayzehr-vay on tahbl
The bill please.	**L'addition s'il vous plaît.**	'ladee-syoñ seel voo play
Waitress/waiter	**Madame, Mademoiselle/ Monsieur**	mah-dam, mah-demwahzel/ muh-syuh
menu	**le menu, la carte**	men-oo, kart
fixed-price menu	**le menu à prix fixe**	men-oo ah pree feeks
cover charge	**le couvert**	koo-vehr
wine list	**la carte des vins**	kart-deh vañ
glass	**le verre**	vehr
bottle	**la bouteille**	boo-tay
knife	**le couteau**	koo-toh
fork	**la fourchette**	for-shet
spoon	**la cuillère**	kwee-yehr
breakfast	**le petit déjeuner**	puh-tee deh-zhuh-nay
lunch	**le déjeuner**	deh-zhuh-nay
dinner	**le dîner**	dee-nay
main course	**le plat principal**	plah prañsee-pal
starter, first course	**l'entrée, le hors d'oeuvre**	l'oñ-tray, or-duhvr
dish of the day	**le plat du jour**	plah doo zhoor
wine bar	**le bar à vin**	bar ah vañ
café	**le café**	ka-fay

Menu Decoder

baked	**cuit au four**	kweet oh foor
beef	**le boeuf**	buhf
beer	**la bière**	bee-yehr
boiled	**bouilli**	boo-yee
bread	**le pain**	pan
butter	**le beurre**	burr
cake	**le gâteau**	gah-toh
cheese	**le fromage**	from-azh
chicken	**le poulet**	poo-lay
chips	**les frites**	freet
chocolate	**le chocolat**	shoko-lah
coffee	**le café**	kah-fay
dessert	**le dessert**	deh-ser
egg	**l'oeuf**	l'uf
fish	**le poisson**	pwah-ssoñ
fresh fruit	**le fruit frais**	frwee freh
garlic	**l'ail**	l'eye
grilled	**grillé**	gree-yay
ham	**le jambon**	zhoñ-boñ
ice, ice cream	**la glace**	glas
lamb	**l'agneau**	l'anyoh
lemon	**le citron**	see-troñ
meat	**la viande**	vee-yand

milk	**le lait**	leh
mineral water	**l'eau minérale**	l'oh meeney-ral
oil	**l'huile**	l'weel
onions	**les oignons**	leh zonyoñ
fresh orange juice	**l'orange pressée**	l'oroñzh press-eh
fresh lemon juice	**le citron pressé**	see-troñ press-eh
pepper	**le poivre**	pwavr
pork	**le porc**	por
potatoes	**pommes de terre**	pom-duh tehr
rice	**le riz**	ree
roast	**rôti**	row-tee
salt	**le sel**	sel
sausage, fresh	**la saucisse**	sohsees
seafood	**les fruits de mer**	frwee duh mer
snails	**les escargots**	leh zes-kar-goh
soup	**la soupe, le potage**	soop, poh-tazh
steak	**le bifteck**	beef-tek, stek
sugar	**le sucre**	sookr
tea	**le thé**	tay
vegetables	**les légumes**	lay-goom
vinegar	**le vinaigre**	veenaygr
water	**l'eau**	l'oh
red wine	**le vin rouge**	vañ roozh
white wine	**le vin blanc**	vañ bloñ

Numbers

0	**zéro**	zeh-roh
1	**un, une**	uñ, oon
2	**deux**	duh
3	**trois**	trwah
4	**quatre**	katr
5	**cinq**	sañk
6	**six**	sees
7	**sept**	set
8	**huit**	weet
9	**neuf**	nerf
10	**dix**	dees
11	**onze**	oñz
12	**douze**	dooz
13	**treize**	trehz
14	**quatorze**	katorz
15	**quinze**	kañz
16	**seize**	sehz
17	**dix-sept**	dees-set
18	**dix-huit**	dees-weet
19	**dix-neuf**	dees-nerf
20	**vingt**	vañ
30	**trente**	tront
40	**quarante**	karoñt
50	**cinquante**	sañkoñt
60	**soixante**	swasoñt
70	**soixante-dix**	swasoñt-dees
80	**quatre-vingts**	katr-vañ
90	**quatre-vingt-dix**	katr-vañ-dees
100	**cent**	soñ
1,000	**mille**	meel

Time

one minute	**une minute**	oon mee-noot
one hour	**une heure**	oon urr
half an hour	**une demi-heure**	urr duh-me urr
one day	**un jour**	urr zhorr
Monday	**lundi**	luñ-dee
Tuesday	**mardi**	mar-dee
Wednesday	**mercredi**	mehrkruh-dee
Thursday	**jeudi**	zhuh-dee
Friday	**vendredi**	voñdruh dee
Saturday	**samedi**	sam-dee
Sunday	**dimanche**	dee-moñsh

Selected Town Index